BARRY DAVIES joined the Welsh Guards in 1962 at the age of 17. Some four years later, he volunteered for the SAS, passing selection while winning the trophy for 'Best Shot'. He remained with the SAS for 18 years, during which service he was involved in skirmishes that covered the globe.

One major event in his SAS career was taking part in the Mogadishu hijack. The British Prime Minister sent Barry Davies and others to assist the German Government rescue of 92 people from the Lufthansa 737. With their direct help the Germans stormed the aircraft, killing three of the four terrorists, while freeing all the remaining hostages. For this action the Queen awarded him the British Empire Medal.

On leaving the SAS Barry Davies turned his writing hobby into a profession. He has written numerous bestselling books about the SAS and produced several television programmes. His recent books include *The SAS Illustrated History*, *The Complete Encyclopaedia of the SAS* and *Operation Royal Blood*. In addition to writing he also travels the world lecturing on anti-terrorist techniques.

Also by Barry Davies

SURVIVAL IS A DYING ART

FIRE MAGIC

GOING HOSTILE

SAS ESCAPE & EVASION

SHADOW OF THE DOVE

SAS RESCUE

SAS SELF DEFENCE GUIDE

THE SAS ILLUSTRATED HISTORY

SAS EMERGENCY MEDIC

THE COMPLETE ENCYCLOPAEDIA OF THE SAS

SAS ENCYCLOPAEDIA OF SURVIVAL

OPERATION ROYAL BLOOD

Barry Davies

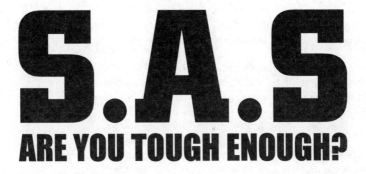

S.A.S
ARE YOU TOUGH ENOUGH?

The Real Story Behind SAS Selection

BⒺXTREE

First published 1998 by Sidgwick & Jackson

This edition published 2001 by Boxtree,
an imprint of Pan Macmillan Ltd
Pan Macmillan, 20 New Wharf Road, London N1 9RR
Basingstoke and Oxford
Associated companies throughout the world
www.panmacmillan.com

ISBN 0 7522 2026 8

5 7 9 8 6

A CIP catalogue record for this book is available from the British Library.

Typeset and colour reproduction by seagulls
Printed by Mackays of Chatham plc, Chatham, Kent

Photographs on jacket and in colour plate section © BBC,
photographer Kieron McClarron
Photographs in black-and-white plate section © Barry Davies

Contents

Author's Note **viii**

List of Illustrations **ix**

Introduction **xi**

1 **SAS History 1**

2 **Preparation 13**

3 **Route Selection 36**

4 **Continuation Training 74**

5 **Survival Training 93**

6 **Fighting in Different Terrain: Jungle/Desert and Arctic 115**

7 **SAS Squadrons 141**

8 **Anti-Terrorist Team 167**

9 **SAS Operations 192**

Index **211**

Author's Note

I should like to emphasize that the chapters relating to real SAS training in this book are taken from personal accounts or that of other SAS soldiers. From time to time SAS Training Squadron change its format and programme to suit the Regiment's requirements, and there could well be slight differences to what I have portrayed. Likewise, this book does not reflect any official views on preparation for SAS selection. For security reasons and to protect those still serving, the training routes have been changed from those used by the SAS.

MOTIVATION, THE DECIDING FACTOR

'When technology has provided the best possible equipment and materials in accordance with the latest scientific theory and the greatest personal experience, when men have been clothed, equipped and declared medically fit, there is still one factor which must be taken into account. This is the human element, and in particular the motives involved.'

Hunt

List of Illustrations

1. Volunteers carry rifles.
2. Off-road vehicle course.
3. Walking up, running down.
4. Volunteer on Point to Point.
5. Good map reading is a must.
6. Dermot O'Leary talks to volunteer.
7. Combat survival.
8. Swimming at the end of Long Drag.
9. Hooded and interrogated.
10. Volunteer is taken for medical check-up.
11. Hot meal.
12. Parachute training.
13. Static line jump.
14. Target recce.
15. Jungle shooting range.
16. Operating in a respirator.
17. Firing a weapon.
18. Briefing session.
19. Two finalists.
20. Candidate on SAS selection map reads.
21. Candidate runs with a bergen.
22. The Story Arms.
23. SAS beret and belt.
24. The Killing House.

25. The M16/203.
26. SAS firing a crossbow.
27. Range work.
28. Air Troop.
29. Room-combat training.
30. Four-man patrol.
31. Captured.
32. Interrogation.
33. Survival kit.
34. Heli-borne assault.
35. Jungle terrain.
36. River-crossing.
37. Lead scout.
38. Military training in Norway.
39. Mountain Troop.
40. Boat Troop.

Introduction

SAS selection is hard, there is no other way to describe it. The basis of the selection system is there to ensure that valuable training time is only spent on the very best recruits. In the dictionary, the word 'select' means 'to pick out the best or most suitable', or 'chosen for excellence'. At Hereford nobody picks or chooses the candidate, they must earn their place – it's more a case of the individual selecting himself.

The programme *SAS – Are You Tough Enough?* was conceived with the idea of selecting a group of civilians and putting them through a ten-day ordeal based on the real SAS selection process. The credit for its conception must go to the BBC producer Graham Cooper. However, not even the BBC has the time and resources to equal real SAS selection in which the cost runs into millions.

It should be emphasized that there is a vast difference between the television volunteers and soldiers who attend a real SAS selection. A soldier attending SAS selection has at least three years' military service, during which he would have learnt the basics such as map reading, weapon handling and most importantly essential foot care. Additionally, the SAS draws heavily on soldiers from the parachute and best infantry regiments – most of whom are at a constantly high level of fitness. Apart from the fitness aspect, most of the television volunteers attempted a military course while lacking fundamental military skills.

SAS – Are You Tough Enough? is not a game show, neither is it a documentary; if anything it is a serious experiment in the facets of human behaviour and endurance. One hundred of the eight hundred applicants who originally applied were asked to attend the fitness test at the BBC gym in London. Of these, thirty were selected and five more were held in reserve. The individual exercises the volunteers performed were very similar to those undertaken by the SAS, but due to time restrictions we had to adapt the exercises for the television programme. A much better idea of what the SAS have to endure is clearly outlined in this book.

Dermot O'Leary was chosen as the series presenter. He played the role of go-between, interviewing both volunteers and participating staff to ensure that the viewing public would get a clear understanding of events. Eddie Stone took on the role of Training Squadron Staff Sergeant and was ably assisted by his four directing staff, known to all as the DS. The Staff Sergeant and the DS had all completed the real SAS selection and served with the Regiment for many years. This small team oversaw the actual running and organization of the various exercises that the volunteers carried out. I was taken on as the behind-the-scenes SAS expert. Having worked for more than a year on the programme my main objective was to ensure that the various exercises functioned correctly and safely. Just as importantly, I made certain that we did not undermine the contribution and work of the SAS.

The SAS regularly use the Brecon Beacons in Wales as training ground for their soldiers, and originally, we had intended to use the Brecon Beacons as the venue for our exercises. However foot and mouth disease forced us to move the site from Wales to The Trossachs in Scotland.

While the production team lived in a nearby hotel at Kinlochard, the newly arrived volunteers were put under canvas in a specially constructed camp. The volunteers were the fittest of the fit: men and women who had proved themselves in a wide variety of extreme sports. We had them all: world record holders, Ironman and marathon winners, mountaineers and fell runners. Most arrived with highly specialized clothing and equipment, together with a keenness to get started. Few realized what was in store for them.

Day one saw the withdrawal of all their personal kit, including the clothes they had arrived in. Each volunteer was given a bergen (an SAS term for a rucksack) and a rifle. The bergen contained military clothing and equipment, sufficient for all their needs. This procedure also ensured that everyone would be competing on equal terms. Eddie and his men carried out this transformation under the sinister glow of camp lights. The conversion brought the volunteers firmly back to reality.

Safety was a real issue. Bad weather and low mist over the mountains can be a major problem. People could fall, get injured or suffer from hypothermia. In part, this problem was solved by the use of individual tracking devices carefully situated in the top of each bergen. These highly sophisticated devices allowed us to observe, on a small laptop computer, the movement of each volunteer as he or she trekked across the mountains.

After a good night's sleep the volunteers seemed ready for our first exercise: Point to Point. The route was to start and finish at Comer Farm and run three times over the trig point at the top of Ben Lomond. The volunteers ran the first leg together but split into red and blue teams at the trig point on the top of Ben Lomond. From there the red team went north while blue team went south, changing over routes on the second leg.

The Scottish route was higher than its counterpart in the Brecon Beacons and the going underfoot was a lot tougher. However the route's distance of 15.5 miles (25 kilometres) compares to that used in the Brecon Beacons, with the volunteers carrying a 35lb bergen plus a rifle. Using Naismith's rule of 5 kilometres per hour plus 30 minutes per 300-metre climb we estimated that this should have taken between six to eight hours. We were wrong. Most of the volunteers were slow and the route had to be restricted to just two legs. Only one man could have completed the whole exercise inside the time but it is clear that others were not as fit or as prepared as we had originally thought. Although the venue differed, I believe the outcome would have been the same had we been in the Brecon Beacons. The weak were dismissed in a daily ceremony where Eddie Stone simply called out their names and told them to get on the truck – after which they were instantly removed. There was no appeal.

At darkness approached the volunteers prepared for their next exercise: Long Drag. The weight they were carrying had been increased to 55lb at this stage and the first major controversy raised its head: should the women carry the same weight as the men? In the end the conflict was resolved by the women themselves. On being told that she would only carry 35lb, one woman volunteer became very disgruntled – she wanted to carry the same as the men. After a somewhat heated discussion it was decided that all the volunteers should carry the same weight.

After four hours' rest with little time for sleep, the volunteers set off on Long Drag. 'Long Drag', also known as 'Endurance', is the final march of the test week for those attending SAS selection. It is a 40-mile (64-kilometre) march over the Brecon Beacons carrying a 55lb bergen and lasting 20 hours. The terrain we used circumnavigated Loch Katrine and is similar to that used by the SAS in the Brecon

Beacons. At 5 kilometres per hour plus 30 minutes per 300 metre climb, I estimated that it should take between 20 and 22 hours.

It was dusk as the sombre volunteers set off. They had no idea how far they had to walk. As they reached one rendezvous (RV) they were given the next. We had planned for the full 40 miles but this turned out to be too far for most of the volunteers. Again, only one man (Karl Webster) looked capable of completing the whole course within the allotted time – he was so far ahead of the field at the 26-mile point that he had to be recalled by helicopter! With time slipping away we collected the weary volunteers and took them to the loch where they were made to swim with their bergens. Dismissals were a solemn affair – the strain was beginning to tell.

Stripped of their bergens and waterproof clothing, the volunteers were each issued with a First World War greatcoat, a sketch map and a survival tin – they were now entering the escape and evasion exercise. Survival instruction was brief and as darkness closed in the volunteers struggled to construct a shelter and build a fire. It started to rain.

The next morning they were up early. As many of the volunteers could not map read and as the weather forecast was looking bleak, we formed them into groups of four for safety. The DS sent them off with a 4-hour start before our search teams gave chase. Looking like a scene from *Colditz*, the volunteers ran (most were hobbling at this stage) into the forest and disappeared. The hunter force was formed from the DS, and men and dogs of the local search and rescue team. We also had a helicopter, but the weather had deteriorated to the point that it was grounded. Despite visibility being down to 30 metres, some patrols managed to reach the RV, while others simply got lost. It was midnight before we managed to round up the stragglers and put hoods on them all prior to taking them to the interrogation centre.

Although no one was physically harmed during interrogation, it must rank as one of the most authentic features of the whole series: so realistic in fact that some of the production team wanted it stopped. Gary Hunter, the series producer, displayed exceptional foresight and interrogation continued. In fairness it was frightening, but it was properly controlled, with a doctor and psychiatrist present at all times. As the nightmare ended for the volunteers, they were lined up and dismissals took place. The decision this time was easy, those caught trying to thumb a lift on the main road were out, and several others had given up during interrogation.

After some hot food in their bellies and a good night's sleep, the volunteers awoke to several new faces – the parachute instructors had arrived. It was time to dispatch the volunteers from 12,000 feet in their first free-fall jump.

The parachute school was very professional and soon our first volunteer was climbing to a height of 12,000 feet. If you have never completed a parachute jump believe me, it takes a lot of nerve. Unfortunately, the cloud base dropped to 3,000 feet and so only one volunteer was able to carry out his free-fall jump. Undeterred, we retrained the rest and gave them a static line jump instead. They loved it. The torment of the previous four days forgotten, the volunteers experienced the biggest adrenalin rush of their lives. Staff Sergeant Eddie Stone tried a little 'beasting' but there was no breaking their spirits. Their jubilation was a wonder to behold, especially that of Cassius Frankson who had previously been scared of heights. Our volunteers were still high as later that same day we took them to the local swimming pool to complete the SAS swimming test, an event which led to more dismissals – including Cassius.

By this time there were eight volunteers left: seven men and one woman. It was now time to see how they would act as soldiers, and so they were formed into two four-man patrols. After a mission brief they were sent off to complete a Close Target Recognisance (CTR). This involved using state-of-the-art surveillance equipment such as night vision aids and covert cameras. Once again the volunteers were tracked throughout the mission, and this time we also monitored their movement on target via closed-circuit television. One of the teams was led by the only remaining woman (Louise Rickard) who, thanks to her army cadet training, did an outstanding job. There were no dismissals at this stage.

The next exercise was to give the volunteers a shot at firing a real weapon. This we achieved, albeit under very different conditions to those used by the real SAS, at the police range in Fife. The result was mixed, but overall none of the volunteers showed much promise. The jungle range exercise had better results, even though we were restricted to using air-soft weapons. The volunteers were taken one by one through some rough and very wet terrain. At certain intervals targets would pop up and the volunteers had to shoot them. As an additional hazard a demolitions team had rigged several booby traps along the route. Everyone was getting tired at this stage and mistakes were being made, so series producer Gary Hunter called a halt to any further exercises, allowing everyone to get a good night's sleep. However before we all headed back to the comfort of our hotel bedrooms, the final four dismissals took place.

The next morning the four finalists set out on their final exercise. They were tasked with capturing a military commander wanted by the War Crimes Commission. Although not part of SAS selection training, this was included to portray the kind of work the SAS are currently involved in. The preparatory work for the finalists and the production team took up most of the day. There would be only one attempt at this and, as dusk fell, everybody gathered for a full safety brief. The scene was set and the exercise began.

The patrol skimmed across the loch and silently approached the beach. A guard at the boathouse is eliminated and the team moves stealthily towards the house. Masks on, weapons ready, Control issues the standby: 'Standby…GO.' The door is smashed open; stun grenades explode; machine guns rattle as room combat drills bring forth cries of 'ROOM CLEAR'. Suddenly they have the target. Down the stairs, out of the door. Guns blazing, they run for the beach. The prisoner and team launch themselves headlong into the waiting boat which speeds off seconds later, leaving little more than a white wash disappearing into the darkness. The exercise ends.

The DS sat down and made a decision as to who was the best volunteer. It was close but overall Gary Robertson had the edge. And so the first *SAS – Are You Tough Enough?* programme was completed. Did we achieve anything? Yes. We made one hell of a brilliant programme. Love it or hate it, it is compulsive viewing. If you think you're tough enough, then start training.

One final word: could any of these people pass the real SAS selection course? In my opinion only a handful had trained hard enough in the six months they had to prepare; equally only the same handful had acquired the necessary map reading skills. No. I do not feel any of the volunteers could have met the challenge of SAS selection. Not because they lacked fitness, however, but because they all lacked a basic military background. The exercises were military and run under military guidelines, but the volunteers were civilians and therein lies the problem, the difference and the final outcome.

As I stated at the start of this introduction, SAS selection is hard. This book covers most requirements for those wishing to join the SAS: how to get fit enough, how to conduct yourself, and what to expect once you enter a squadron. It

also highlights some of the reasons for joining – the exciting action-packed life, the exhilarating travel experiences,
and not forgetting the SAS specialist pay. The book also
gives you a full picture of life in a regiment which, in our
world of terror, has become one of the most respected and
feared special forces units ever.

CHAPTER ONE

SAS History

In the world of Special Forces, whether they are used in war or counter-terrorism, one name in particular stands above the rest: the Special Air Service SAS. Originating in World War II as a 'renegade' unit, it has since developed an awesome reputation based upon its bravery, skills and professionalism. The SAS soldier is trained to the peak of his potential: the ultimate definition of a professional warrior.

The SAS is used primarily for putting down insurgencies, or for special missions behind enemy lines, such as was seen recently in the Gulf War. To date, one of their most effective and most public roles has been their use of direct action against terrorism.

In 1940, David Stirling was a lieutenant with No 8 Commando. In the belief that a small band of dedicated men could operate successfully behind the enemy lines, he managed to present his plan to General Richie, who at the time was Deputy Chief of Staff. His idea and memorandum finally reached the Commander in Chief of the Middle East, General Auchinleck, and the SAS was born. As the founder of the SAS, Stirling's main strength came from his ability to select and enlist men who had both daring and vision. One such man was Paddy Mayne. Mayne was one of Stirling's first recruits into the SAS, the nickname 'Paddy' came with his Irish ancestry. Before the war he was well known for his accomplishments in the world of sport. In battle he possessed qualities of leadership, which set him apart from most men; he was awarded four DSOs.

The SAS patrols first fought in the North African desert in World War II. They used the American Willy, a jeep that was light, agile and robust, ideally suited to desert conditions because of its four-wheel drive. Fitted with 0.5 Browning heavy machine-guns or twin Vickers 'K', originally used by the RAF as an aircraft gun, they would load up with fuel or water before driving hundreds of miles to attack the Germans behind the lines. These hit-and-run raids were highly successful, especially in destroying vast numbers of enemy aircraft.

Later on, men of the first SAS were parachuted behind German lines to support the Normandy landings. During several of these operations, many men were captured by the Germans and executed. Hitler realized that the SAS were very dangerous and issued orders that all members were to be executed when captured.

The birth of the modern day 22 SAS, came into being because of the communist troubles in Malaya between 1950 and 1959. In the early 1950s, a British officer, Mike Calvert, who was serving in Hong Kong at the time, was instructed to appraise the communist influence in Malaya. Calvert, a tough soldier who had commanded an SAS brigade during the last war, innovated the idea of the Malayan Scouts (SAS). He instigated many of the basic tactics that exist today, the most famous being the four man patrol. They performed and operated under very hostile conditions in enemy territory. The Malayan Scouts formally became known as 22 SAS and Calvert instructed John Woodhouse to return to England to set up a formal selection course. The concept of that original selection course has changed little, although much more is expected of the modern-day SAS candidate.

As the SAS established itself as a regular British unit, the tasks set them grew thick and furious. Between 1959 and 1967 the SAS were active in Borneo and Aden. Of these, Jebel Akhdar in 1959, was the scene for a daring SAS operation. Some seventy men from D Squadron, were transported directly from the jungle to the desert, where they immediately went into action. During the assault on Jebel Akhdar, a young Captain by the name of Peter de la Billière won the Military Medal for his actions.

The role of the SAS during the Aden conflict was limited to up-country patrolling and a 'Keeni-Meeni' unit which would operate in the towns. The SAS found it difficult to come to grips with this conflict because of the deteriorating political situation and the number of enemy factions involved.

By 1970, the Oman war had erupted and the SAS were back to their fighting role again, supporting the new Sultan against the communist backed Adoo guerrillas. By this time, the Keeni-Meeni patrols had developed into the Counter-Revolutionary Warfare (CRW) unit at Hereford. This was mainly due to the rise in terrorism both at home and inter-nationally. While Northern Ireland soon became the proving ground for CRW training, the anti-terrorist team, known originally as the SP team, was set into motion to combat international terrorism. The SP team remained fairly secret until such headline makers as the Mogadishu hijack and the Iranian Embassy siege. Despite such media coverage, the SAS still maintained their combat capabilities, as was seen during the Falklands War. Even here, many of their actions went unreported to the general public.

During 1991, the world watched as the Gulf War unfolded, bringing new and wondrous weapons to the theatre of war. Stealth bombers and 'smart' bombs gripped the world's imagination. The SAS was used along with other special forces on clandestine missions, but their role only really became known after the war was over. In a reprise of the SAS's original task, patrols were sent deep behind enemy lines, at great risk, to gather intelligence, hunt Scud missiles and to sabotage equipment and the war-machine infrastructure. These were 'low-tech' operations that often had as much success, if not more, than the vaunted 'high-tech' weaponry much beloved of the media.

More recently, the SAS have been involved in other roles. In Albania they were called upon to rescue a British couple who ran an orphanage as well as the children who lived there. This was achieved with maximum efficiency and minimum fuss and was a successful mission, even though the couple and children decided to return to the orphanage a few days later. In Bosnia, as part of the peace-keeping efforts, the SAS has been involved in the arrest of war criminals. Their actions made the headlines in July 1997 after they shot dead one of the men they were arresting. The man, Simo Drljaca, upon being challenged, pulled a gun on the soldiers and shot one in the leg. It was this imprudent action that cost him his life.

There is no doubt that the SAS will continue to be Britain's elite fighting force for many years to come. Who knows: there might be a place for you among the pages of its as yet unwritten history.

SAS LIFE

If you have a reputation for fighting in your parent unit, I suggest that you lose it before you get to Hereford. The SAS prove themselves on the Brecon Beacons and on operations, not in bars. Fighting is considered a sign of bad discipline in the SAS, as is scruffiness and lack of punctuality. Getting stupidly drunk and misbehaving, even if it is a minor offence, will mean an immediate return to unit, even if your record on operations is otherwise excellent. Being RTU'd from the SAS is one of the worst things that can happen. If it does happen, take it on the chin and hope that one day you will be allowed back in. This has happened and many have done better the second time around.

The popular 'gung-ho' image of life in the SAS does not bear much relation to the facts. Although the role of the regiment is continually changing, and the 'uniform' seems to be one of 'civilian dress', never forget that all SAS men are soldiers, first and foremost. Like other soldiers in the British Army they are required to serve at times with other units and attend military courses outside of Hereford. Such courses may require you to wear uniform and may involve saluting, or standing on parade and doing local regimental duties. A good SAS soldier will take all this in his stride. You must also learn to respect the views of other soldiers in the British Army, many of whom are equally tough physically and just as mentally adept. You must understand that people hold different opinions and that these should be accepted, even if you disagree. On the other hand, don't believe everything you see or hear – not everything can be taken at face value. While it's OK to be relaxed, you must participate and learn from your instructors, that is why the regiment sent you there in the first place. I completed many external courses during my eighteen years at Hereford, and many I found extremely interesting, but if someone were to ask me to sum up the skills of an SAS soldier, I would say he was a Jack-of-all-trades, and master of most.

SAS Tip: the glamour that surrounds the SAS – the secret operations, the distinctive badge – can sometimes arouse feelings of envy, dislike and misunderstanding in others. If you come across someone with these feelings, it is better to avoid him, rather than try beating his head in. Sometimes a very rewarding and fun way of dealing with someone who has a grudge against you is to be super nice to them – they get really confused.

Don't let the fact that you are badged SAS go to your head. In Hereford, you are just a small cog in a very large machine. You will encounter other units of the army, most of which are involved with supporting you. They are often looked down upon, or dismissed as unimportant. This is not so in the SAS. You must recognize that these so called 'crap hats' are an essential part of a fighting army. Bear in mind that without the signals guy sitting at his desk your messages will not get through. The army chefs not only cook your meals at Hereford, they also travel abroad with the regiment, if you upset them or treat them with less respect than they deserve, you may find yourself eating crap. As an elite fighting soldier, you are no more important than the logistics, intelligence or communications personnel who support you. Without them, you will be going nowhere.

Self-discipline is the most important discipline in the SAS. The code of self-discipline has taken nearly fifty years to establish, so that each man knows what is expected of him. There is a great interdependency between officers, NCOs and troopers; anyone who is not dependable, no matter what his rank, will be binned. When you are new to the regiment, a good tip is to listen to what the officers have to say – many started out as troopers, and what they don't know is not worth hearing. One interesting part of SAS life is that most senior NCOs remain with the regiment and get commissioned.

COURAGE

The SAS have become part of a modern mythology – new heroes for this age winning battles and achieving daring feats.

Although some of the stories are true, others have become so distorted by the media that they bear little resemblance to the truth. Little wonder then that the public often has a complete misconception about who the SAS are and what they do. They can be portrayed as super-heroes, or on some occasions, gun-toting yobs – their missions becoming acts of glory or acts of unwarranted aggression.

The truth is rarely heard, as the SAS has a policy of keeping quiet on most things. But one thing is certain: the history of the SAS is full of true stories of bravery, both physical and moral, performed by men who were not super-heroes or super-thugs, but just professional soldiers getting on with what they were trained to do.

Many recent books go on about the courageous episodes the SAS have achieved. Courage is an important attribute in the SAS and the following pages contain examples of extreme courage shown by men in desperate situations. There are two types of courage: physical courage, and, more importantly as far as the SAS is concerned, moral courage. Physical courage alone can often cause a man to act foolishly in the face of danger for fear of otherwise looking cowardly. In this type of situation, that courage is more a product of pride or ego – the man will be less worried about any danger and more worried about what others will think of him. This sort of attitude is not desirable in the SAS.

Moral courage is rarer and tempers bravery with wisdom. This trait ensures greater chances of survival in any situation as decisions are based upon common sense rather than ego or fear of criticism. A man with moral courage will not only work well in a team, but also by himself – he doesn't need praise and flattery to keep going. This type of person will be able to cope with most predicaments – even capture and interrogation by the enemy – and end up with an even greater strength and self-respect.

So what makes these elite soldiers risk their lives? There are probably many reasons, but the first and foremost is the protection of our 'freedom'. In much of the Western world, this concept sounds old-fashioned and something we all take for granted. But let me tell you, I have fought in many parts of the world, where oppression, death and destruction are treated as normal. World politics are extremely complex and few people realize that what happens in a far-off country can affect our own. Sometimes it is difficult to understand why our soldiers have to go and take part in someone else's conflict, but politically there is always a good reason.

The SAS have been involved in many such foreign conflicts, and sometimes a story will reach the public back home and become part of the mythology. The following incidents help to illustrate typical SAS bravery. Before you arrive at Hereford, read these and ask yourself, 'Could I have done that?'

When Peter de la Billière was colonel of the Regiment he made several changes to the way in which selection was taught, fearing that good soldiers were failing due to excessive standards imposed by the DS. Another of his very wise decisions was to decree that every soldier passing into the Regiment would purchase and read Lord Moran's *The Anatomy of Courage*.

THE BATTLE OF MIRBAT

On 19 July 1972, just before dawn, a battle took place at the port of Mirbat in the Dhofar province of Oman that was in every way as astounding as Rorke's Drift. A group of SAS soldiers, heavily outnumbered by enemy forces, managed to hold their position until relief forces arrived. It was a remarkable feat by any standards and the outcome seriously damaged the morale of the rebel forces.

At this time, in the Port of Mirbat, a nine man Special Air Service civil action team was stationed in the town, training local forces and providing basic medical care for the local community. They had made as their base a house located on the outskirts of the town, between the Wali Fort and the Dhofar Gendarmerie Fort. This house became known as the BATT house (British Army Training Team house) and it became a vital command post in the battle that was to follow.

At 5 a.m. on 19 July, a formidable force of about 250 Adoo (the Arabic word for enemy) approached the port from the north. Their first obstacle was the Gendarmerie picket on the top of a small hill called Jebel Ali. They had intended to take this post by surprise but a single shot rang out as they were spotted by a sentry and a gunfight ensued.

Alerted by the sound of small arms fire, the SAS BATT team immediately appraised the situation and saw that the sound was coming from the direction of the Jebel Ali. At first it seemed like little more than a stand-off attack, and the commander of the BATT team, Captain Mike Kealy, shouted orders for the 81mm gun to be opened up in support of the beleaguered Gendarmerie picket. At the same time, the big Fijian, Labalaba, ran the 500 metres to a gun pit just outside the Gendarmerie Fort. This pit contained a 25-pounder artillery piece left over from World War II, a crucial weapon in what was to occur. Captain Kealy, as a safeguard, radioed to SAS Headquarters at Um al Quarif to relay information about the situation. Meanwhile, the other members of the team took up positions behind sandbagged emplacements.

Suddenly the town itself came under attack from a vast amount of small arms fire. The shadowy figures of the Adoo were now advancing on the perimeter wire from the direction of the Jebel Ali. Immediately, both machine-gun bunkers, the 81mm and the 25-pounder opened up on the attackers. Before long, Labalaba radioed the BATT house to inform them he had been hit on the chin and his countryman, Takavesi, volunteered to go to his aid. Kealy readily agreed, knowing that Labalaba would not have reported a trivial injury. Under covering fire, Takavesi dashed to the gun pit and found Laba, field dressing on his wound, still firing the gun. The big man, ignoring his injury, indicated the unopened ammunition boxes and the need to keep firing.

Takavesi decided to try and get some help from the DG Fort and ran the few metres to the door. Eventually his frantic banging was heard and an Omani gunner, Walid Khamis, answered it. Together they ran back to the gun pit, but just as they reached it, Walid was hit in the stomach by a bullet and fell, badly wounded.

The DG fort was now being hit by rockets and was slowly being pounded apart. From the roof of the BATT house, Kealy could see that the Adoo had now breached the perimeter fence and were advancing in waves. He had already called for air-strike support, but the chances of that were pretty dismal as the cloud cover was low enough to make such an operation extremely dangerous. He watched in despair as the Adoo moved ever closer to the fort and the gun pit.

By now, the 25-pounder was firing at point-blank range into the charging attackers. Suddenly Takavesi was hit and slumped back against the sandbags. Despite being badly wounded, he picked up his SLR and continued to fire at the enemy. Not long after, Laba was hit too, this time fatally in the neck. Upon losing communication with the gun pit, Kealy and an SAS medic, Trooper Tobin, decided to move forward to render assistance to the gun pit, despite the risk. Kealy made another desperate call to HQ for back-up and a casevac chopper. The two men then worked their way forward under heavy fire.

When they reached the pit they discovered just how grave the situation was: Laba lay dead, and Takavesi and Walid were badly wounded. Tobin assessed his priorities and immediately went to work, setting up a drip for Walid. Meanwhile, Kealy and Takavesi continued their desperate defence of the pit, picking off Adoo as they appeared at its edge. The fighting was fierce, and Tobin was caught in the face by a bullet. He fell, mortally wounded by the side of the big Fijian, Laba.

All seemed lost when suddenly there was a huge explosion: the SOAF Strikemaster jets had arrived, despite the low cloud. The jets, with their heavy cannon, drove the Adoo into a large wadi just outside the perimeter fence. There, they dropped a 500 pound bomb on them. Meanwhile, more relief had turned up in the shape of SAS G Squadron, which by luck had been based only a short distance away. Upon hearing of the BATT team's plight, twenty-two of them, under the command of Captain Alastair Morrison, assembled an impressive array of weapons, loaded themselves on to three choppers and made the thirty mile journey in ten minutes. Due to the low cloud they had landed to the south of Mirbat where they instantly met with an Adoo patrol. Needless to say, this was quickly neutralized.

Members of G Squadron engaged the enemy in short running battles. The Adoo were soon in retreat, leaving behind thirty-eight dead, countless wounded and taken prisoner. At last it was safe enough for the casevac helicopters to land. The first to be taken out were Trooper Tobin and Walid Khamis. Takavesi was also seriously wounded and covered in blood but was still managing to raise a smile. In fact, his wounds were such that a normal man would have died, but his courage was so great that he insisted on walking to the chopper without assistance.

Back at Mirbat, Captain Alastair Morrison reorganized its defences and set about the task of collecting the Adoo dead and wounded. In comparison with the Adoo numbers, of thirty-eight dead and over fifty wounded, the SAS had lost two, with two seriously injured; the Gendarmes had lost one man with one injured, and the Omanis had one man dead.

The attack on Mirbat was the last great attack by the Adoo in the war and its failure left them completely demoralized. A proud warrior people, they had been humiliated by defeat when the odds were so heavily in their favour. They lost some of their best men in that battle. They could not have known that a second SAS squadron was so near or that the SOAF pilots would have shown such nerve and expertise. Above all, they could not have predicted the bravery of the men dedicated to holding the gun pit at whatever cost to themselves.

In more recent times of trouble, such as the Gulf War, new stories of rescue emerged. The story of 'Bravo Two Zero' and 'The One That Got Away' both tell different accounts of a patrol isolated in the middle of the Iraqi desert and being hotly pursued by the enemy. The patrol had been inserted by chopper, deep behind enemy lines. Their mission was to observe the movement of Iraqi Scud missiles that were threatening Israel. Almost immediately, they were discovered by the enemy and engaged in a fire-fight. The patrol then made a run for the Syrian border. Hunted every inch of the way, travelling in adverse weather conditions, they laid waste to over two hundred Iraqi soldiers. The outcome was that one man made it, three died, and four were captured. The latter were tortured but released at the end of the war.

These are just a few events where SAS men have risked, or given their lives to help others. There have been many other individual accounts, and doubtless there will be many more in the future. On operation, SAS men trust each other implicitly. It is the cornerstone that sets them apart from others. Think about these stories before you think about joining the SAS. Could you have committed yourself as these men did?

CHAPTER TWO

Preparation

SPECIAL FORCES BRIEFING COURSE

The SAS now run several weekend courses, which give a lot of information to potential candidates for Special Forces selection. Many soldiers arrive at Hereford totally unprepared; this serves as a disadvantage to both the individual and the Regiment. Those attending will get a brief insight into the role of Special Forces, a physical assessment and good advice on getting fit.

JOINING INSTRUCTIONS FOR SFBC

Students will be told how to find their way to Sterling Lines and what time to arrive, this is normally between 1600 and 1700 hrs on a Friday evening. Those travelling by train need to take a taxi, indicating that the driver should take them to the Main Gate Sterling Lines, they all know where it is. For those arriving by car, make sure to do so in plenty of time as you will need to book your car in at the guardroom on arrival.

Make sure you have your MOD Form 90 (Identity Card) with you, and a copy of joining instructions. You will also need a Fit for Course Certificate or F Med 566 signed by your unit medical officer stating you are fit enough to attend the course.

All students are required to confirm their attendance with

Training Squadron before joining the SFBC. If the dates are not suitable, then students should get their unit clerk to liaise with Training Squadron and arrange an alternative.

COURSE FORMAT

The idea behind the SFBC course is to ensure that prospective candidates are fully aware and prepared before they attempt Special Forces selection. It is also an opportunity for the Regiment to look at you, to make sure they like what they see.

You will be given a series of briefings and presentations, about the role of British Special Forces in general and specifically that of the SAS. This normally kicks off with a brief from Training Squadron OC. Next you will be briefed on what selection is all about and how best to prepare yourself, the weekend normally goes as below.

Friday evening

Brief	Map Memory Test
TOETS	Military Knowledge Test
Map Reading Test	IQ Test
First Aid Test	

Saturday

Before breakfast you will do an APFA and a Bleep Test. After this you will be taken to the swimming pool where you will be required to jump off the high diving board. This is to assess your initial aptitude for parachute training. To be honest I have never quite worked out how they calculate this – just jump into the water to pass. During your visit to the pool you will also be required to swim 100 metres in 3 minutes, after which you must tread water for 10 minutes, all this is done in combat clothing and trainers. For the rest of the morning you will receive briefings on the Regiment, which include not just the combat side but also such subjects as welfare and daily living at Hereford.

In the afternoon you will be driven to a training area to the south of Hereford where you will carry out a series of fitness tests, these include BFTs (Battle Fitness Tests) and CFTs (Combat Fitness Tests). The BFT is straight forward, and the first CFT consists of running 2 miles in 18 minutes, the second is 8 miles in 1 hour 40 minutes. All these tests are done back to back, none are particularly difficult but make sure you stay close to the leading group, don't fall back.

Saturday ends with a briefing on the activities of Special Forces detailing some of their specialist roles. You may get the opportunity to have a few pints on Saturday night, make sure it is a few.

Sunday

The DS will make you run for about one and a half hours, during which time you will be required to carry other students. These exertions will include both the fireman's lift and baby carry, feats you must do going both uphill and downhill. When you are not carrying another student you will be sprinting.

Once you have survived the fitness training, you can relax by watching the Regimental video, which gives a rather glamorous laid-back image of the SAS. Before dispersal around lunchtime, you will receive a final interview: as I said at the start of this passage, watch how you perform, they are watching you, if they don't think you're SAS material, you won't be coming back to Hereford.

DRESS AND EQUIPMENT FOR THOSE ATTENDING SFBC

DPM (Disruptive Pattern Material) Combat Suits, lightweights are best. You will require two sets, one of which is used for swimming.

Boots – 2 pairs. (Do not use the new flat surface boot; make sure the boot has a heel.)

Training shoes – 2 pairs. (One is used for swimming.)

Normal unit working dress.

Civilian tracksuit and running shorts – 2 sets.

Bergen (It is advisable to prepack your bergen with a weight of 35lbs.)

Sleeping bag.

Helmet Mk 6 type.

Belt with water bottles – 2.

Notebook, pens etc.

Washing and shaving kit.

There are no special SAS secrets to passing selection: there is only reality. This reality comes down to your age and how well you have prepared yourself prior to arriving at Hereford. Your chances of passing are a great deal less if you are over thirty, or spend most of your day in a sedentary occupation, for example behind a desk or driving a tank. A good standard of fitness can only be achieved by hard work – there are no short cuts. There is a great deal of truth in the saying: 'No pain, no gain.' You may see some candidates at Hereford who think that they have found 'magic formulas' and short cuts to make them better performers. These hypochondriacs bring with them all sorts of vitamin pills, supplements and concoctions, believing them to be superior to a good training routine and diet. Don't follow this route. Remember, a good breakfast is far better than a handful of vitamin pills.

This chapter covers the standard of fitness required and

how to achieve it. Prior to arriving at Hereford for selection, it is essential that the candidate undertakes a hard-working, self-imposed training schedule. To build up energy, a good calorie-rich diet is also recommended. Other skills can be learnt prior to selection, and these should be practised during this build-up period. For example, learning to read a map and compass accurately will help you navigate well during selection, particularly when visibility is poor. And talking of visibility, an understanding of weather will also be helpful when you are on the Brecon Beacons.

HOW FIT ARE YOU?

Ask yourself how fit you are and how long it will take you to prepare. You should be making this decision long before you apply to join the SAS. The old saying, 'life is what you make it', is true. I have always believed that everyone can do what-ever they want to in life as long as they are motivated. If you have your health, your physical state and level of fitness are in your own hands.

> **SAS Tip:** I once knew a lady, aged about thirty-five, who worked for an International drugs company. The clarity of her eyes was the first thing you noticed. The second thing was her peach-like skin. When I asked her how she managed to stay so beautiful, she replied, 'We are what we eat.' This lady virtually ate nothing but fruit. She was also a keen hill walker and could keep up with the best.

Being physically fit and healthy depends very much on your mental attitude. Determination plays the largest part, but lifestyle is also extremely important. Getting through SAS selection is directly related to fitness and the soldiers that do get through reach a standard of fitness that will last them for years. After selection, the continued training and lifestyle of the SAS soldier carries on with this process, honing his body and mind to their peak of performance. If you don't believe me watch how some of the older DS (Directing Staff) seem to fly around the Beacons with ease.

FOOD

Food is the fuel that feeds our body and keeps us going. It provides the building blocks for growth and repair. What you eat will have a direct effect on how your body performs, on your health, and how long you live. In the normal course of events people watch what food they eat to control their weight and achieve an attractive figure. Well, forget about counting the calories. Eat what you want. It is advisable to eat a mixture of foods so that your body gets an even supply of proteins, fats and carbohydrates.

Eating is one of the more pleasant daily functions of life. Food offers a wonderful variety of taste, texture and smell, and the kitchen at Hereford is staffed by some of the best chefs in the army. During selection, eat and enjoy all the food you can cram into your stomach, 2500 calories are the normal intake for an active man, but you should eat 4000–5000 calories at least.

SAS Tip: Breakfast is the most important meal of the day, so don't skip it for the sake of an extra half hour in bed. On long marches, get as much food down you as possible before you start and make yourself some egg and bacon sandwiches for when you are on the move. Remember to eat before you start to get tired though, for a physically exhausted body will begin to reject food and you will end up being sick.

IMPROVING YOUR FITNESS

There is only one person who knows the true level of your fitness and whether you stand a chance at passing selection, and that is you. The average SAS soldier works hard at keeping himself fit and constantly compares himself to his colleagues. For a start, it is vital to be honest with yourself . . . how fit are you really? Define this and then work out a target. Next, examine your daily routine, diet and lifestyle, both in barracks and at home. Drinking and late nights may have to be sidelined for a while. Also, take your age into consideration; you may have the greatest mental determination to pass, but is your body up to it?

CHECKLIST FOR FITNESS

- Do you exercise?
- Could you run ten miles at a steady pace, keeping your breathing under control?
- Could you walk ten miles over hilly country, with a 20 kilo rucksack?
- Do you drink more than two pints of beer, or the alcoholic equivalent each day?
- Do you have high blood pressure?
- Does your diet contain a regular supply of high-fat foods?
- Is your weight comparable with your height?
- Do you smoke?
- Do you take drugs?
- What is your work routine?

A candidate coming from a parachute regiment or infantry unit will most likely be fairly fit, but you don't have to come from these units to be in the SAS. Age is a very important factor. Men are at their peak of fitness between 21 and 25. In this age group most soldiers are naturally fit. Between the ages of 26 and 30, fitness begins to lessen as daily work and the marriage routine take their toll. This does not mean that fitness cannot be maintained. Over the age of 30, it gets harder to maintain a good level of fitness, but you can still try out for selection – many men over the age of 30 have successfully completed it and become members of the Regiment.

WARM UP

Learning to warm up properly, especially before you start any exercise, is very important. This should be part of your aerobic exercise and need only take a few moments. Setting off cold will increase the possibility of damage to joints and muscles. A good technique is as follows: Start by deep breathing. Fully exhale, then inhale slowly to the count of ten. Exhale also for ten counts. Repeat this three times. The purpose of this is to increase the amount of oxygen being delivered to the muscles, which in turn produces energy. Oxygen is vital for the body to function properly. One of the most important things I have learnt about exercise is that the body needs fresh air. To give you an analogy, I once asked a farmer friend why he was watering his potatoes when it had been raining non-stop for the past few days. His answer was that the common spud would absorb any amount of water, thus improving its size and weight. Similar principles apply to the human body and its intake of air.

Whenever an SAS soldier finishes selection, he is as fit as he will ever be – he will literally glow. This is because the hard, mountainous terrain of selection causes much forced breathing, which in turn gets a lot of fresh air into the body. The oxygen is absorbed by the blood which then feeds it to the muscles and brain, creating extra strength, stamina, energy and alertness.

> **SAS Tip:** do your warm-up exercises the moment you get off the trucks, they only take a few moments. Do not wear your bergen while doing warm-up exercises.

Touching Your Toes

Stand upright and stretch your arms into the air above your head. Bend your knees bringing your arms down in front of you and between your legs. Return to the standing position. Repeat 5 times.

Squats

Lower yourself from the standing position to a squat; then stand up. Keep your back straight. Repeat 5 times.

Knee Hug

From the standing position, keep your balance while you pull your left knee up to your chest. Hold the knee in position for a few seconds, before releasing and repeating with the right leg. Repeat 3 times with each leg.

Lunge Stretch

With your feet slightly apart, bend your knees then stretch backwards with one leg, while bending the other knee. At the same time raise your elbows above your head, forcing them backwards slightly. Repeat 3 times with both legs.

TRAINING ADVICE FOR POTENTIAL STUDENTS ON SF SELECTION

This programme is aimed at potential students who wish to attend SAS selection. You should start preparing yourself at least six months in advance, this will allow you the maximum chance of passing the course.

Always warm up and stretch before exercise. Eat a good breakfast, and drink plenty of fluids *not alcohol!* Take good care of your feet by taping up potential blister hot-spots and keep toe nails trimmed. If you develop an injury stop and seek medical advice. If you are unable to run for a few days due to injury concentrate on your swimming. *Do not over train.*

TRAINING DEFINITIONS

All runs should be preceded by a half-mile warm-up jog. Ideally this should be done on a flat, grassy surface. Running takes many forms:

Jogging Dress warmly and run at a pace where you can hold a normal conversation.

Normal Rate Run at the same pace making sure you can maintain a steady rhythm with your breathing, this should be between 70 and 80 per cent of best effort pace.

Best Effort Run as fast as you can.

Hill Repetitions Find a steep slope, which takes no more than a minute to sprint to the top of, or mark off a start and finishing point on a long incline. Sprint up the hill, then jog down to recover. Build up from 1 repetition to 3 repetitions.

Repetition Training Run at best effort for 1 minute, jog for one minute. Start by doing this 3 times, building up to 6 of each. Once you can run and jog comfortable for 1 minute intervals, increase the distance to 90 seconds and so on.

Orienteering This involves running around a set route using a map and compass. You should introduce this type of training into your programme at the earliest opportunity.

March The SAS terminology for walking with a bergen over the hills. Try to maintain a steady pace walking all the time. Do not be tempted to run down hill during your build up training, it is the easiest way to injure yourself.

TRAINING PROGRAMME

Week 1

Monday	3 mile jog
Tuesday	Rest
Wednesday	5 mile jog
Thursday	Swim 10 lengths
Friday	Rest
Saturday	5 mile jog
Sunday	Rest

Weeks 2 and 3

Monday	5 mile jog. Swim 15 lengths in the afternoon
Tuesday	5 mile jog
Wednesday	3 mile best effort
Thursday	Swim 15 lengths. Jog 3 miles in the afternoon
Friday	20 hill reps
Saturday	3 mile jog
Sunday	Rest

Week 4

Monday	Swim 15 lengths. 3 mile jog in the afternoon
Tuesday	Simple circuit training
Wednesday	Rest
Thursday	Repetition training, about 5 miles
Friday	Swim 15 lengths
Saturday	Rest
Sunday	Rest

Week 5

Monday	6 miles (steady). Swim 20 lengths in the afternoon
Tuesday	Circuit training. Hill repetitions in the afternoon
Wednesday	5 mile jog. Swim 20 lengths in the afternoon
Thursday	Circuit training. 5 mile jog in the afternoon
Friday	5 mile jog. BFT in the afternoon
Saturday	8 miles normal run
Sunday	Rest

Week 6

Monday	5 mile jog. Circuit training in the afternoon
Tuesday	Swim 25 lengths. Hill repetitions in the afternoon
Wednesday	5 mile jog. 5 miles in the afternoon
Thursday	Swim 25 lengths
Friday	5 mile jog. Circuit training in the afternoon

Saturday	8 mile normal run
Sunday	Rest

Week 7

Monday	Swim 20 lengths. 5 mile normal run
Tuesday	5 mile jog
Wednesday	Rest
Thursday	5 mile normal run. Circuit training in the afternoon
Friday	5 mile normal run
Saturday	Rest
Sunday	Rest

Week 8

Monday	Swim 30 lengths. 5 mile normal run and circuit training
Tuesday	Hill repetitions. 5 mile jog in the afternoon
Wednesday	6 mile march with bergen (35lbs) 1hr 15 mins (*do not run*)
Thursday	3 mile jog
Friday	Swim 30 lengths. 8 mile normal run in the afternoon
Saturday	10 mile march with bergen (35lbs) 2hrs
Sunday	6 mile march with bergen (35lbs) 1hr 15 mins

Week 9

Monday	Rest
Tuesday	Hill repetitions. 5 mile normal run in the afternoon

Wednesday	Circuit training. 3 mile jog in the afternoon
Thursday	Swim 35 lengths
Friday	Rest
Saturday	10 mile march with bergen (35lbs) 2hrs (*do not run*)
Sunday	10 mile march with bergen (35lbs) 2hrs (*do not run*)

Week 10

Monday	Rest
Tuesday	5 mile normal running.
Wednesday	Swim 30 lengths.
Thursday	Rest
Friday	BFT and circuit training.
Saturday	Rest
Sunday	10 mile march with bergen (35lbs), 1hr 50mins (*do not run*)

Week 11

Monday	Rest
Tuesday	5 mile jog. Circuit training in the afternoon
Wednesday	Orienteering in the hills. Aim to cover 20 miles with a 45 lbs bergen
Thursday	3 mile jog. 8 mile march with bergen (30lbs) in the afternoon, 1hr 40mins
Friday	Orienteering in the hills. Aim to cover 20 miles with a 45 lbs bergen
Saturday	5 mile jog
Sunday	Rest

Week 12

Monday	5 mile march with bergen (35lbs), 1hr
Tuesday	BFT
Wednesday	Rest
Thursday	3 mile run best effort.
Friday	Rest
Saturday	Rest
Sunday	8 mile normal run

Aim to take a two-week break between finishing your training and attending Hereford. This will give the body time to rest and any blisters time to heal.

A FEW THINGS TO REMEMBER WHEN YOU ARRIVE AT HEREFORD

- Keep your mouth shut.
- Always do exactly what the instructors tell you, do not argue.
- Be grey, let them notice how well you are doing naturally.
- If someone asks your opinion, give it clearly without any bullshit; if you don't know the answer just say so.
- Do not try to cheat, the DS know every trick in the book.
- When you are exhausted and think you can't go on, slow down, but keep moving.
- Take strength from every person who falls by the wayside, while he is being RTU'd, you will continue.
- Do not skip meals. Eat all you can, you'll need the calories.
- Do nothing that will bring you to the attention of the instructors. If they don't like you then you'll probably fail even though you pass the other criteria of selection.
- When walking in a group with the DS; do not try to

overtake him, do not click at his heels, best stay within range of the lead group, but at the back.

- Do not follow the pack unless you are convinced they are going the right way.
- Study the map; study the ground; study your compass. Know where you are at all times.
- Arrange your water supply so that you can drink on the move.
- Always have your rifle in your hand or immediately next to you.
- Remember why you came here in the first place; you came to *pass* SAS selection.
- Do not take a walkman on selection. Not only will the DS be highly displeased, but it also means you will not be concentrating on your route.
- If you make it through to continuation there is a very good chance you'll remain in Hereford.

BERGEN

It is vital that you get used to carrying a bergen (rucksack) around before you reach Hereford. Your bergen contains everything you need to survive – shelter, sleeping bag, clothes, food and water. It is like carrying your home around, and like a well-kept home, everything should be serviceable, clean and in its place.

On selection, you will be issued with a bergen as well as other items that you will need. First of all, check all your equipment for damage; if there is any serious problem, get a replacement. The first few days, when you are in a group controlled by an instructor, get used to the feel of your new bergen. Check if it is causing any pressure spots, soreness or irritation and adjust it accordingly. If needs be, add padding.

The bergen's centre of gravity should be high on your back and its weight should be distributed between the shoulders and the hips 60/40 respectively. This way, your legs will help to bear the weight and your back will not get strained. Some soldiers use chest straps to stop the bergen bouncing, and while these serve a purpose, I would say they are restrictive for the routes taken on selection.

Packing a bergen is also an important skill and one that should be learned before selection. The most important aspect is deciding what is essential and what is non-essential. Pack a bergen well, and not only should you have what you need, but you will also have greater comfort when carrying it.

> **SAS Tip:** if you are not used to living out of a bergen, here are a few bits of advice to help you. Be warned: on arrival at Hereford, you will see some candidates packing and repacking their bergens – don't do it. There is only one tried and tested method that works and that is based on the principle that you can get to your equipment with the minimum of effort.

- Items needed during your movement should be in the side pockets, i.e. water, brew kit and snacks.
- If you intend to use some form of camel hydration system, again, fit it into one of the side pouches.
- Items needed for foul weather should be kept inside the bergen top flap.
- Place items you only use at a given time in the bottom of your rucksack, sleeping bag etc., with those items that you will frequently use closer to the top.
- Rain soaks into material and makes it heavy. You could end up carrying several extra pounds in a rainstorm. Waterproof your bergen, seal all clothes and porous items in plastic bags.

CLOTHING AND HYGIENE

Man is a tropical animal and needs clothes to protect himself against the weather in most parts of the world. The human body functions best between 96° F and 102° F, above or below that, the person may start to decline in health. Therefore, the maintenance of body temperature and the prevention of injury are just as important to a survivor as the finding of food and water. Body temperature can be affected by climatic temperature, wind, moisture loss, illness and shock. Heat loss or gain can be caused by conduction, convection, radiation, evaporation, respiration and wind.

> **SAS Tip:** from my own experience, the worst threat in any survival situation is wind chill. In cold and wet conditions it can rob the body of heat and in hot conditions it can rob the body of moisture. Do whatever is possible to prevent it.

Soldiers are now issued with the latest in protective clothing, but long term wear and tear will take its toll on any clothing, no matter how good it is. If you allow dirt to build up on your clothes, it will destroy the fibres and reduce the effectiveness of the garment. It is essential to keep your clothes clean. Washing them is the best way. If this is not practicable, a daily shaking or beating will do. Clothes exposed to warm, humid conditions, such as in the tropics, or close to the body will need frequent washing and daily attention otherwise they will rot. This is especially true of socks and underclothing, whose cleanliness is also essential to your health and hygiene. Many native tribes clean their clothes by simply beating them against rocks. If you choose to do this, take care of any buttons and zips that may be damaged.

KEEP CLOTHING DRY

When clothing gets wet, for example through perspiration or rain, its insulation properties become reduced and it will lose heat up to twenty-five times faster than dry clothing. If the wet is then combined with wind, a swift death may be the result. Therefore it is essential to keep clothes as dry as possible. During physical exertion, ensure that there is some ventilation. If they do get wet, make every effort to dry them. This can be done by draping them over clean rocks warmed by the sun, or by hanging them from tree branches. If it is tactically possible, build a fire and dry them by that, but never leave them unattended or else you might burn them. Take especial care when drying leather boots or gloves by a fire; leather, if dried too fast, has a tendency to stiffen and crack.

> **SAS Tip:** in sub-zero temperatures, wet clothing can be hung up to freeze. The moisture turns into ice particles that can then be beaten out. This works best with tightly woven garments. Also, if you manage to fall into water, roll around in powdery snow as this will 'blot up' the wet.

REPAIR

The Eskimos have a very good habit of repairing clothing as soon as it becomes damaged, thereby reducing any further deterioration and maintaining the garment's effectiveness. It is good to adopt this bit of wisdom, especially where windproof garments are concerned. Another tip is to never cut up your clothing for the sake of comfort. In hot climates, don't cut the bottoms off your trousers in order to make shorts.

LAYER SYSTEM

In cold conditions, one of the most tried and tested solutions to keeping warm is to use a layer system. This traps warm air close to the body by using several thin layers of clothing instead of just one thick one.

Your underclothes, that is, those next to your skin, should be made of a thin, cotton material – something like a loose-fitting thermal cotton vest. This layer will absorb perspiration, thereby removing excess moisture from the skin. It is important that this layer is changed daily and washed.

The next layer ideally should be a garment that can be fastened at the neck and wrists, thereby trapping the warm air – for example, a Norwegian-type sweater.

A third layer should consist of a fleece-type jacket that can be easily removed when the body begins to overheat.

Finally, choose an outer garment that is wind and, if possible, waterproof. This could be made from tightly woven cotton, polycotton, fibre-pile material or nylon. It should be fitted with a good hood protecting as much of the head and face as possible. Garments made from such materials as Gore-tex are excellent as they allow trapped vapour to permeate through the fabric, and reduce overheating.

OVERHEATING AND SWEATING

Even in cold weather it is possible to overheat, especially while wearing layered clothing. Blood flow helps to distribute heat round the body, so be aware of any tight or restrictive clothing that may hinder this blood flow. If you're wearing more than one layer in the case of gloves and socks, make sure that the outer layer is comfortably large enough to fit over the inner. If you find yourself overheating, first of all, loosen the clothing at neck, wrists and waist. If this isn't enough, start to take off your outer layers of clothing, one layer at a time. As soon as you stop exercising or working, you should put these clothes on again or else you will become chilled. If the weather is wet remove one of the inner layers, always maintaining a waterproof outer layer.

The most important points to remember are:

- Keep clothes clean
- Avoid overheating and sweating
- Keep clothing dry
- Repair defects immediately
- Improvise.

GOOD FEET AND FOOTWEAR

A healthy pair of feet and good footwear are major requirements for those attending selection. The fact that we carry our entire body weight on two feet instead of four, like other animals, means that we place pressure on those feet. This is especially true on selection when we are also carrying the additional weight of a heavy bergen as well as walking over rough terrain. It is important that you look after both your feet and your boots. Failure to do so could easily mean not getting through selection, no matter how fit the rest of you is. Always wear clean, dry socks and be aware of the condition of the skin around your feet. *Remember, during selection, your feet are your only transport.*

DEALING WITH BLISTERS

Normally, blisters are considered a minor injury and treated as such. However on selection, the pain of a blister can become disabling out of all proportion to its medical significance. Blisters on selection are usually caused by ill-fitting boots, poor quality socks or loose laces combined with long periods of having to walk over rough, uneven ground.

Bad blisters can be avoided. First of all, the feet must be kept clean and dry – washed whenever possible, dried thoroughly and foot powder applied. If you notice sore spots on your feet while you are training, put some surgical spirit on them to toughen them up.

As soon as you feel a blister beginning, stop immediately and treat the problem. Put some antiseptic cream on the sore area and then cover it with surgical dressing, without making any creases in the tape. If the sore area is on a toe, use micropore tape instead. If a blister has already formed, use a blister ring so that pressure is kept off the affected area.

A severe blister is often filled with fluid, and can be made more comfortable if the fluid is removed. To do this, do not burst it, as this leaves a larger area open to infection, but pierce it at the bottom edge using a sterilized needle. If possible, wash the foot thoroughly first. Then gently express the fluid and cover with a blister ring as described above. Make sure that the dressing is changed daily and the area cleaned. A footbath of hot salty water is healing, comforting and helps to harden the skin. However, make sure that the area is thoroughly dried: blisters heal best when they are kept clean and dry.

SAS Tip: blisters can be extremely painful, even more so when the feet are cold. On selection, you may not have time to attend to them. If this is the case, close your mind to the pain and carry on. The pain will still be there but once your feet have warmed up it will become bearable.

BOOTS

It is a mistake to come to selection with a brand new pair of boots. It is far better to choose a pair that your feet have become accustomed to, as long as they are in good condition. I recommend a good lightweight combat boot manufactured in high quality leather with a high-grip rubber sole.

> **SAS Tip:** pay attention to what the DS are wearing and how they are dressed. Listen to their recommendations for different weather conditions.

LOOKING AFTER YOUR BOOTS

To get a long life out of your boots, look after them well. Always clean mud from them at every chance then wash and polish them. Any detachable insoles and wet laces should be removed and dried thoroughly using either the sun or other heat source. Beware though of putting boots too close to an open fire as leather tends to crack when it dries too fast. Once the boots are dry, apply several layers of a good waterproof compound, making sure that each layer is well rubbed in.

Using gaiters on selection is a good idea as they can keep your boots dry. When snow is on the ground, they may keep most of it from going down your boot, or when crossing rivers they may keep the worst of the water out. Two types of gaiter are available: those that clip over the laces and those that fit over the whole boot.

CHAPTER THREE

Route Selection

This is probably the most important chapter in this book, as it shows similar routes to those used during SAS selection. However, it must be noted that many different routes have been used by Training Wing over the years. One thing that never changes is the type of route – they are picked for being a measure of physical endurance and are extremely arduous.

When you are pushing yourself to the limit, both mentally and physically, being able to navigate as if it were second nature is a real must. Not only will it help you through selection but it will stand you in good stead for the rest of your SAS career. Learning to use a map and compass and gaining a good understanding of the terrain is essential. With practice, you will be able to look at a map and visualize the contours and routes in 3D form in your head. This is particularly useful in poor visibility or at night.

> **SAS Tip:** the basic map reading course I took on Salisbury Plain was one of the most instructive and useful courses I have ever done. I am convinced the skills I learned there afforded me a great advantage and helped me to pass my SAS selection.

MAP READING

The correct use of a map and compass is a basic skill that every soldier can build upon until he is fully competent in navigational techniques. Other navigational skills, not dependent on a map and compass, can also be learned and are extremely useful in survival situations. These basic skills can also prove useful if your compass or GPS gets lost. For example, during the endurance march of my selection I lost my compass and was forced to use the miniature one from my survival tin. It was extremely difficult to see it at night and my fingers got frozen just holding it – but it got me to the finishing point.

MAPS

Maps vary in size and design, so take care and choose the right one for the job. Soldiers are usually issued with Ordnance Survey maps that have a scale of 1:50,000. Pilots, on the other hand, are given maps with a larger scale, detailing a wider area. Survival maps, usually issued for operations behind enemy lines during war are generally printed on cloth instead of paper. In most cases you will be issued with a 1:50,000 map for use on selection. Fold your maps with care, protect them in a map case or waterproof bag sealed with tape. *Do not write on the map or mark it – ever.*

SETTING THE MAP BY INSPECTION

Look for an obvious and permanent landmark, for example a river or a mountain. Find the feature on the map and then simply align the map to the landmark.

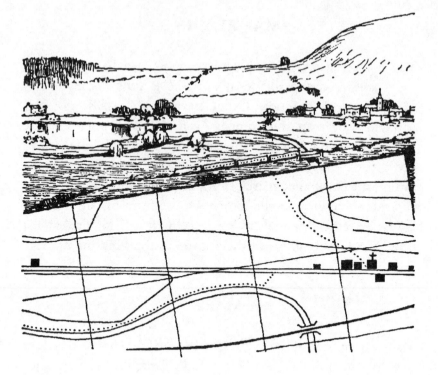

Setting the map by inspection

SETTING THE MAP BY COMPASS

Pick a North–South grid line on your map and lay the compass, flat, along it. Then, holding the map and compass together, turn both together until the compass needle points North.

FINDING A GRID REFERENCE

When you look at the map, you will see that it is covered in horizontal and vertical light blue lines. These are called grid lines and are one kilometre apart. The vertical lines are called

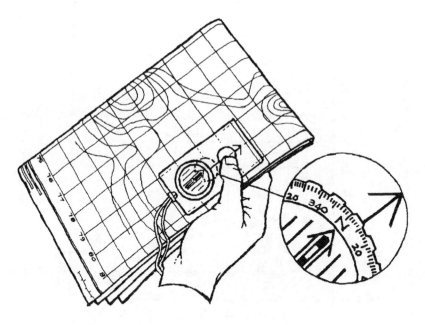

Setting the map by compass

eastings: these are always given first. The horizontal lines are called northings; these are given after the eastings. Each grid square is defined by the numbers straddling the left grid line of the easting and the centre bottom of the northing. For example, the illustrated grid square reads 2853.

Usually, a grid reference contains six figures. This is worked out in the following way: the grid square is mentally divided up into tenths, for example half way up or across a square would be '5'. This reference point is then added after the relevant easting or northing figure. To gauge the tenths accurately, use the romer on the compass, or a protractor. The grid reference of the railroad bridge is 286535.

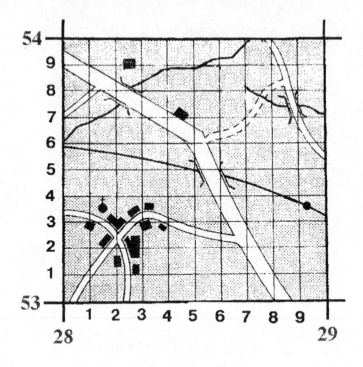

Finding a grid reference

TO TAKE A COMPASS BEARING FROM THE MAP

Once you have established where you are and where you wish to go, work out your route. Study the map and the distance. Plot the most logical route to your objective, taking into account the terrain and any obstacles. Divide your route up into legs, finishing each leg close to a prominent feature if possible, i.e. a road bridge, trig point, of even the corner of a forest area. Take a bearing from where you are (call this point A) to the feature at the end of your first leg (call this point B). Place one edge of the compass along the line adjoining A and B making sure that the direction of travel arrow is pointing in the way you want to go. Hold the compass plate firmly in position and rotate the compass dial so that the lines engraved in the dial are parallel to the North–South grid lines on the map. Finally, read off the bearing next to the line of the march arrow. To walk on this bearing simply keep the magnetic arrow pointing North and follow the line of the march arrow.

The bearing gives the direction to a certain point. It can be defined as the number of degrees in an angle measured clockwise from a fixed northern gridline (easting). The bearing for North is always zero. Most compasses have scales of 360 degrees, or more normally they are shown in mils with 6400mils in a circle. Some compasses have both.

KEEPING ON COURSE

Three factors will determine which route you take: the weather, the time of day, and what the terrain is like between you and your final destination. In good visibility select features that are both prominent on your map and visible to the eye. Once you have taken a bearing, choose a feature along the line of march and head towards it. This saves you constantly looking at your compass. It will also help keep you on course if the terrain pushes you off track, i.e. you are forced to contour or avoid some obstacle. Success on selection is having confidence in your route selection, and not becoming a slave to your compass. Mistakes in poor visibility can be avoided if you consult the map every time you meet a prominent feature. Careful study of the map should provide you with a mental picture of the ground relief which will in turn warn you of any obstacles, such as river or marshland.

SAS Tip: the Brecon Beacons are extremely steep, and there is a tendency during fog or poor visibility to wander downhill when you are contouring. Every hundred metres

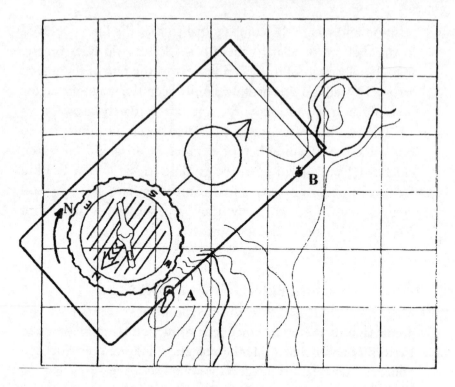

To take a compass bearing from the map, rotate dial until the North indicator is in line with the North/South grid lines. Read off the bearing by the direction of travel arrow.

or so take a few steps uphill to compensate for this. Don't forget that you will move slower in poor visibility.

MAGNETIC VARIATION

When we talk about 'North', bear in mind that there are three Norths. True North is not generally used in navigation; it is the fixed location of the North Pole. Grid North is more familiar – it is the North shown on maps by the grid lines.

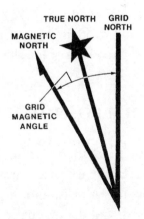

Magnetic Variation

Magnetic North is where the needle on the compass always points due to the strong magnetic attraction generated by the Earth's magnetic field. However, the direction of magnetic North may vary by a small fraction from year to year due to changes in this magnetic field. This difference can be calculated using the information shown on the map, i.e. the date it was printed and the degree of variation. This variation is then either added or subtracted to Grid North to get a more accurate bearing. Put simply: Mag to Grid, get rid; i.e. subtract the variation from your compass bearing before applying it to the map.

Grid to Mag, add; i.e. add the variation to your map bearing before applying it to your compass.

SAS Tip: during selection, shorten the legs of your route. The magnetic variation is so small as to be insignificant over a short distance. This will save you seconds trying to work out the variation and stop you making an error. Some will decry me for saying this, but I have never bothered to work out the magnetic variation when walking. There are normally sufficient features to help keep you on course, although it is advisable to adjust the variation when plotting long routes across barren land or travelling by vehicle.

FINDING YOUR POSITION BY COMPASS

If you become disorientated here is a simple way to pinpoint your position. Find a landmark that can also be identified on the map. Point the compass at it, and, holding it steady, turn the housing until North and the magnetic needle line up. Now read off the bearing to the landmark. For example, say the bearing was 5700 mils, calculate the magnetic variation, which is 40 mils, and subtract. This leaves us with a revised bearing of 5660, for which the compass dial can be adjusted. Placing the top right-hand edge of the compass against the landmark point on the map, turn the whole compass until the magnetic needle is pointing North in agreement with the map. Draw a line. Find another landmark and repeat the whole procedure. For example, the second bearing is 0650 mils, 0610 mils after adjustment for the magnetic variation. Draw another line as above. Your position is marked where the two lines cross.

GPS (GLOBAL POSITIONING SYSTEM)

This new and high-tech method of navigation is worthy of a mention, as I have recently purchased one and found it rather good. Developed by the United State's Department of Defence, the GPS system consists of twenty-four military satellites which orbit the earth, continually giving out the time and their position. This information is picked up by a hand-held receiver unit on the earth. Receiving and assimilating information from several satellites, the receiver unit is then able to fix a position and attitude at any point on the earth's surface. Most special forces and pilots are now issued with GPS navigational aids.

Receiving units vary, as do their accuracy. A deliberate error, called Selective Availability (SA) was built into the system. This dithers the signals so that only a Coarse Acqui-sition (CA) can be obtained, therefore reducing accuracy to about 40 mils. The SA can be overridden for military use by a 'P' code and this gives an accuracy of about 10 mils. P code receivers are very costly and are not available for civilian use. All users of GPS systems, however, can experience P code type accuracy during times of heavy military activity, when the SA is switched off.

HOW IT WORKS

The GPS receiver unit searches for and then locks on to any satellite signals. The more signals you receive, the greater the accuracy, but a minimum of four will do. The information received is then collated into a usable form; for example, a grid reference, height above sea level, or a longitude and latitude. Individual requirements for use either on land or at sea can be programmed into the unit.

By measuring your position in relation to a number of known objects, i.e. the satellites, the receiver is able to calculate your position. This is called satellite ranging. It is also able to update your position, speed and track whilst you are on the move and can pinpoint future waypoints, thereby taking away the need for landmarks.

SAS Tip: the GPS requires tuition in its proper use, as it is not a compass in the strictest sense. In the UK, I have found two models with good instructions: the Silver and the

Garmin 40. The only way to learn either is to get out and practice. Despite its excellent qualities, the GPS system can be shut down, additionally the unit also eats batteries, so don't forget your compass.

DIRECTION FINDING WITHOUT A COMPASS

Compasses may be the easiest and most convenient method of finding a direction, but what if you are without one? During the escape and evasion phase of selection you are most certainly going to be without a compass. Don't worry: there are a few other methods of finding direction. All that is needed is a bit of intelligence and maybe some sticks and stones.

THE SUN

Stick and Stone Method

a. On a sunny day find or cut a stick about one metre long and push it upright into some level ground. The stick will cast a shadow.
b. Using a small stone, mark the end of the shadow as accurately as possible.
c. After fifteen to twenty minutes the shadow will have moved. Using the second small stone, mark the tip of the new shadow.
d. On the earth, draw a straight line that runs through both stones. This is your East-West line.
e. Put your left foot close to the first stone, and your right foot to the second stone. *You are now facing North.*

Note: the accuracy of this method depends on how level the ground is, how well the ends of the shadows are marked, and how much care was taken in placing the toes at the line. A North–South indicator can be produced if a line is drawn at right-angles to your East–West line. Any other direction can be simply calculated from these cardinal points.

USING A WATCH

Northern Hemisphere

Check that your watch is accurately set to local time and then point the hour hand at the sun. This can be made more accurate by using a thin twig to cast a shadow along the hour hand. Bisect the angle between the hour hand and the 12 o'clock position and this line will be due South. North being the end of the line furthest from the sun.

Southern Hemisphere

In the southern hemisphere, the numeral twelve on the watch face should be pointing at the sun. The North-South line is found midway between the hour hand and the 12 o'clock position. However, as opposed to the northern hemisphere, North will be the end of the line nearest to the sun. Again, accurate time setting is essential.

To help confirm which end of the line is pointing North, remember that before Noon, the sun is in the eastern part of the sky, and after Noon, the western. This means that if you are facing North, the morning sun will be on your right-hand side and the afternoon sun on your left.

THE STARS

Navigation by the stars has been used for centuries, and is still employed in map making. Learning about the stars is beneficial in itself, but this knowledge comes into its own in survival navigation.

Bright stars that seem to be grouped together in a pattern are called constellations. The shapes of these constellations and their relationship to each other does not alter. Because of the earth's rotation, the whole of the night sky appears to revolve around one central point and using this knowledge can help you to find directions.

THE NORTHERN HEMISPHERE

In the northern hemisphere, the central point is marked by a faint star, called Polaris, the Pole, or the North Star. Because of its position, it always appears to remain in the same place – above the North Pole. As long as Polaris can be seen, the direction of True North can be found.

To find Polaris, first locate the constellation known as 'The Plough' or 'The Big Dipper'. The two stars furthest from the 'handle' always point towards Polaris. Take the distance between the two stars and then follow a line straight for about six times that distance. At this point you will see the Pole Star. If you are unsure which way to look or wish to confirm that you have found Polaris, look for another constellation called Cassiopeia. The five stars that make up this constellation are patterned in the shape of a slightly squashed 'W'. It is positioned almost opposite the Plough, and Polaris can be found midway between them. As long as the sky is clear, the Plough, Cassiopeia and Polaris remain visible in the sky all night when seen from any country north of 40 degrees N. latitude.

THE SOUTHERN HEMISPHERE

Unfortunately there is no star that is fixed above the South Pole, but it is still possible to locate South in the southern hemisphere by using the stars. The constellation to look for here is the 'Southern Cross': four main stars in the shape of a cross, with a fifth, fainter star just a little way below the centre of the cross. If you take a line through the longest axis of the cross and extend it South for about four and a half times its length, you will come to the approximate position of where a South Pole star would be. To make sure you have drawn a line through the correct axis, check that it runs through a small group of faint stars just as it leaves the constellation. When you have located South, note a landmark directly below this position to give you an easier point of reference. Alternatively, take the bearing you require and lay a stick on the ground as a pointer. In this way you will be able to determine your required direction in the morning.

THE STAR MOVEMENT METHOD

If the sky is partially clouded over, and you are unable to find or identify the major constellations, there is another method you can use. As mentioned earlier, the stars appear to revolve around the sky about one certain point. By observing how the stars are moving, you will be able to gain a rough indication of which way you are facing. To ascertain which way they are revolving, set two sticks in the ground and aim them at any bright star, like you would the sights of a gun.

If the star seems to:

a. Loop flatly towards the RIGHT, you are approximately facing SOUTH.

b. Loop flatly towards the LEFT, you are approximately facing NORTH.
c. be RISING, you are approximately facing EAST.
d. be DESCENDING, you are approximately facing WEST.

THE MOON

Reasonable results can also be obtained navigating by the moon, although I must stress they are only reasonable. Here are two methods:

The Quarter Moons

With either of the quarter moons, you can project a line through the horns down to the horizon. If you are in the northern hemisphere, the place where the line touches the Earth will be approximately South. If you are in the northern hemisphere, it will indicate North. Tests have shown this to be a rough, but useful guide when travelling at night.

The Quarter Moons and the Full Moon

Using your watch, set it accurately to the local time. Phases of the moons are always found at certain directions at certain times. Using this knowledge, and the table below, you can get a good idea of direction.

Time	First Quarter	Full Moon	Last Quarter
1800	South-east	Not visible	Not visible
2100	South-west	South-east	Not visible
0000	West	South-east	
0300	Not visible	South-west	South-east
0600	Not visible	West-south	

VEGETATION TIPS TO NAVIGATION

Plants will often give a general, but not accurate idea of direction, and this should be borne in mind if you are in an area that supports vegetation. Trees will have larger foliage on the sunny side, which in the northern hemisphere is the south side, and north in the southern hemisphere.

Many wild flowers, but especially those with open yellow cups, turn towards the sun wherever it is in the sky, even on a cloudy day. Take note that the wind may be moving the plants. Moss prefers damp, shaded conditions, and therefore grow on the northern aspects (in the northern hemisphere) of trees and rocks, where they receive the least sun. In summary, mosses give an opposite indication of direction to other plants.

PREVAILING WINDS

In desert areas, where local guides to navigation are sparse, try to learn or observe the prevailing wind direction. Prevailing winds are responsible for shaping the sand dunes so that the shape of the dunes can provide a very rough and ready guide to direction.

THE IMPROVISED COMPASS

An improvised compass can be made out of any suitable small metal object, e.g. a needle, pin or a razor blade, provided that it can be magnetized and suspended to swing freely as a pointer. To magnetize the metal, take a magnet and stroke it along the metal in one direction. Note that this pointer may need re-magnetizing from time to time.

When using thread to suspend the pointer, you may find

that it either becomes twisted or that it is too stiff. Either way, the free movement of your pointer will be impeded. In the case of a small, sharp pointer, such as a needle or razor blade this can be overcome by floating it on water. To do this, push the pointer through something that floats, such as a piece of cork, or two or three matchsticks, and let it float on still water in a non-metal container (metal will affect the pointer magnetically). The pointer should now be able to swing freely. Note: the loudspeaker of any radio, even the smallest one, will contain a permanent magnet that can be used in compass making. Looking out for ways in which any object can be adapted or improvised from its original use is the hallmark of a successful survivor.

Electricity can also be used to magnetize a steel pointer. For this you will need a length of insulated copper wire as can be found inside most electrical equipment, and a battery that will produce six volts or more. At these low voltages, the insulation on the copper wire may often only be a coat of varnish.

Making as many turns as you can, wrap the wire around the pointer and then connect it to the battery. After 15 to 30 minutes of current, the pointer will become magnetized, with the North Pole of the pointer nearest to the negative battery terminal (remember – N for North and Negative).

These are just a few of the methods that you can use to navigate in a survival situation. Some of them depend upon knowledge or skill, others upon observation, but all are of value.

INFORMATION ON THE BRECON BEACONS

The Brecon Beacons, located in South Wales, is where most of the selections take place. The mountains are not high, but adverse and changeable weather conditions can make them dangerous. Exposure and hypothermia are constant threats and soldiers have been known to die. Before you arrive at Hereford I recommend that you obtain an Ordnance Survey map of the area and study it (Landranger 160). My advice is to concentrate on the large empty areas to the west and east of the Story Arms. If you get the chance, spend a weekend walking over the mountains. Nothing too strenuous, but get familiar with them. In summer it is an extremely pretty place, especially the river valley that runs through the centre.

TIMINGS

You will hear a lot of the students going on about timings. Don't let it get to you, just do your best. Time is everything on selection but the SAS do not expect you to do the impossible. In summer the ground is dry, and the good going means better and shorter times are achieved. In winter, the wind and rain will slow everyone down. Don't complain, the DS know exactly how long it should take in all conditions and the time allowed will be adjusted to suit. Just to be on the safe side here are some helpful hints to save minutes:

- Drink on the move, using some form of camel pack. (This allows for your drinking water to be in your side pouches and connected to your mouth via a plastic intake tube.)
- Select the fastest route by studying the terrain and contours. This will save you time.
- Be aware of the ground where you will be walking. Even if flat, it may contain a bog which will slow you down, especially if you are tired.
- Do not eat a large meal during the marches; instead try to eat little and often and on the move.

- Check your location continuously so that any mistake can be quickly corrected before you have gone too far in the wrong direction.
- Always keep a little energy in reserve. You never know what the DS have in store.

KIT LIST TO CONSIDER PRIOR TO ATTENDING SELECTION

Good boots and boot care equipment

Spare maps (the 3D type is best for initial training as they show better relief)

Spare compass

Woolly hat (black or green. Don't buy the three-hole ski mask)

Watch, with illuminated dial. (TK from BCB)

Thick elastic bands

Cloth fibre masking tape

Map case

Fablon

Superglue

Waterproof bergen liners, large and small

Comms cord (black)

Para cord

Good brewing mug and plastic spoon

Gaiters

Waterbag container (Jungle and LUPs)

Swiss Army knife

THE FOLLOWING LIST OF EQUIPMENT WILL BE ISSUED TO YOU AT SENNEYBRIDGE CAMP

Prismatic compass

Mini flares, one pack

Weapon key allowing you to draw a rifle from the armoury

Bliss homing device, this must be attached to your bergen

Torch

Mess tins

Emergency rations

Waterproof jacket

Waterproof trousers

Bergen

High visibility panel (fits on top of bergen)

Bivi bag

Sleeping bag

Survival suit in black plastic
    container

Waterbottle, carrier and mug

Maps 1: 50,000 scale (5)

Maps Issued

Brecon Beacons (sheet 160)
    (Sennybridge)

Black Mountains (sheet 161)

Elan Valley (sheet 147)

Hay on Wye (sheet 148)
    (Radnor Forest)

Forest of Dean

INITIAL SELECTION ROUTES

The routes on the following pages are similar to the ones used
on SAS selection – the real routes cannot be revealed for
reasons of security. However, these will still give a realistic taste
of what the student can expect.

Day 1

The course begins with every student going through a combat
fitness test. Range road 148 at Sennybridge is normally used,
with the course being split up into two groups. (At this stage
the numbers are very high). You carry 30lb bergens, belt kit
and a rifle; the pace is very fast. Your bergen is weighed before
you start and a rock added if you are under weight (food and
water do not count as weight). Try to finish somewhere in the
front group, and look relaxed at the end, the DS will want to
see you looking switched on.

Day 2

Get ready for the Fan Dance. This starts at the Storey Arms where you are placed in a group and given a colour, each group will have its own DS. You carry a bergen weighing 40lb, belt kit and rifle. You should remember to warm up by stretching before starting, also try to relax; much is made of the Fan Dance but it is not that hard. The DS will race off, keep him in sight but don't burn yourself out trying to catch him, even if you do he will be pissed off. You need to finish the Fan Dance inside four hours to pass, try for less if the weather is good.

Day 3

Day three is in Sennybridge Camp where you will be instructed in map reading, make the most of this. In the afternoon you will get a one-hour beasting with loads of push-ups, fireman's lifts etc.

Day 4

What remains of the course is divided into two groups, half will take a swimming test while the others do physical training on the football pitch. The latter is hard, loads of shuttle runs, crawls, push-ups, and carries. In the afternoon you will be taken to Radnor Forest area where you will again be split into groups each with its own DS. This is basically a map reading exercise at speed; you carry 40lb bergens, belt kit and rifle. The DS use small 'sickeners' such as running up steep hills or making you carry extra weight.

Day 5

You are taken to Brecon swimming baths where you will swim 20 circuits of the pool. (Stay to the outside, do not try to cut corners and distance.) This is done wearing shirt and trousers, belt, and a full water bottle. You must also complete one width under water and be able to tread water for 10 minutes. Directly after this you return to Radnor Forest and repeat the map reading exercise of the previous day. An evening meal is supplied via containers before you set off on your first night march. A sample route is as follows:

Start point Road Lay-by Grid 0175 1060
RV1 Bridge Grid 9450 1120
RV2 Pot-Hole Grid 8910 1615
Finish point Road Junction Grid 844 164

Once completed you will have time to crawl into your green maggot and get some sleep. You will be woken around 5.30 a.m. and given a container breakfast.

Day 6

After your night march you are driven to the Forest of Dean for an orienteering course, for this you will be paired off with another student. (Use the travel time to get a bit more kip.) The course consists of six waypoints around the forest, all of which are fairly easy, that said the DS will harass you to make better time. 30lb bergens are carried.

Day 7

You rise at 7 a.m. and are taken out to Sennybridge training area where the DS will beast you rotten for about two hours.

Stay with it, show the DS you are hanging in there and can take a lot more. You return to camp and are normally stood down until Monday morning. Have a beer but don't get drunk, stuff your face with protein.

Day 8

Have a lie in. Check your clothing for wear and do repairs. Check your boots and feet. Get an early night's sleep. You will get a brief that evening on the next day's activities.

Day 9

Parade at 7 a.m. where you will get your colour for the day and be told which truck to get on. You will be taken to the Elan Valley, use the travel time to sleep. At the start point you will have your bergen weighed before being given your first grid reference. Make sure you know and understand exactly where you are going. The route will be around 15km and will take about 4 hours 30 minutes. A similar route in Radnor.

Start point Road Junction Grid 1080 6465
RV1 Trig-point 538 Grid 1705 6065
RV2 East end of Pool Grid 1400 5940
RV3 Telephone Box Grid 1255 5820
Finish point Road/River Bridge Grid 1140 5445

Day 10

You do more or less the same procedure as for day 9 but with a different route. You will have a 40lb bergen and be required to finish the route in about 4 hours 30 minutes. Distance 20km.

Start point Pub Car Park Grid 8810 2915
RV1 Standing Stones Grid 8335 2835
RV2 Standing Stones Grid 8360 2570
RV3 Spot-height 591 Grid 8475 2315
RV4 Spot-height 562 Grid 8620 2065
RV5 Spot-height 582 Grid 9080 2640
Finish/start point Grid 8810 2915

Day 11

Still in the Radnor area, 40lb bergen, 14km. Typical route:

Start point Telephone Box Grid 172 585
RV1 Spot-height 523 Grid 193 609
RV2 Trig-point 660 Grid 182 639
RV3 Spot-height 491 Grid 159 635
RV4 Trig-point 538 Grid 171 606
Finish/start point Grid 172 585

Day 12

Rest day. The DS will give you pointers on what and where you have been going wrong, and you will receive a briefing on test week.

Day 13

Radnor Forest with a 45lb bergen, distance 29km in about six hours.

Start point Road Junction Grid 160 647
RV1 Spot-height 491 Grid 159 636
RV2 AA Box Grid 198 598
RV3 Trig-point 610 Grid 214 636

RV4 Stream Junction Grid 202 671
Finish/start point Grid 160 647

Day 14

Day off. Rest up and get ready for some really serious work.

Day 15

'Pipeline' is a 23km march over the Brecon Beacons with a 50lb bergen. It is hard. Typical route:

Start point Lay-by near Dam Grid 987 198
RV1 Spot-height 632 Grid 938 186
RV2 Pot-Hole Grid 891 161
RV3 Trig-point 725 Grid 881 191
RV4 Trig-point 603 Grid 912 216
RV5 Spot-height 632 Grid 938 186
Finish/start point Grid 987 198

Day 16

'Point to Point' is 25km with a 50lb bergen.

Start point Lay-by Grid 972 222
RV1 Pen-V-Fan Grid 012 216
RV2 Car Park Grid 024 249
RV3 Pen-V-Fan Grid 012 216
RV4 Track Junction Grid 034 182
Finish/start point Grid 972 222

Day 17

'Heavy Carry' means a 70lb bergen. This is extremely difficult. You start off with a 50lb bergen but after a short time you are made to carry a twenty pound ammunition box full of concrete; this weight is additional to your rifle, belt kit, water and rations. The distance is around 15km. Typical route:

Start point Road Junction Grid 773 259
RV1 Stone Circle Grid 808 244
RV2 Trig-point 802 Grid 826 218
Finish point Road Junction Grid 861 246

Day 18

'Endurance,' or 'Long Drag' is a real bitch. All I can say is if you have made it this far it is worth putting your all into this final march. You have to walk 40 miles over the Brecon Beacons with a 55lb bergen in 20 hours. You will start around midnight with little or no sleep between the previous day's march and Endurance. Sleep on the truck if you can, every little helps. Typical route:

Start point Road Junction Grid 080 260
RV1 Track Junction Grid 034 182
RV2 Fan Fawr Grid 964 189
RV3 Trig-point 603 Grid 913 216
RV4 Road Track Junction Grid 868 193
RV5 Ystradfelle Reservoir Grid 944 073
RV6 Road Bridge Grid 995 164
RV7 Track Junction Grid 034 183
Finish point Grid 080 260

Author's Tip: each time you approach a RV make sure you

do so in good order, that is to say, look fresh, no clothes hanging off you; carry your weapon correctly. Give your colour code and number i.e. 'Williams, blue route two, Staff.'

If asked where you are show the DS by pointing with a blade of grass or the corner of your compass; don't use your finger. When you get told the next grid indicate it on the map, the DS will only tell you twice. Move away and plan your next leg. Look confident.

Day 19 and Onward to Jungle Training

Well, if you make it this far give yourself a pat on the back. You will be taken back to Hereford where you will be given a much deserved long weekend break. When you return on the Monday you will be integrated with new members of the SBS who have passed their initial selection course. At this stage you will be formed into four man patrols, normally two SAS and two SBS. You will practise patrol techniques and ambush drills ready for the jungle phase. You will also learn how to handle the M16, Claymore mine and how to operate the PRC 319 radio. For those who are not familiar, detailed instruction is given on using a One-Time Pad (OTP) for encrypting messages.

It is good advice to get yourself into the jungle before you attend selection. The advantages of having served time in jungle conditions are of enormous benefit. That is not to say that those attending the jungle phase will fail, some students take to the jungle as if it were their natural habitat, others find it claustrophobic. A short posting to Belize or a course at the jungle training school will stand you in good stead. If you cannot do this, see the section on jungle terrain later in this book.

EQUIPMENT ISSUED FOR THE JUNGLE PHASE

Tropical shirts	2
Tropical trousers	2
Sweat rags	2
Black floatation bag	1
Blanket	1
Poncho (green)	1
Tropical hat	1
Hammock	1
Hammock poles	6
Machete	1
A frame cover	1
Water bag	1
Ammo pouches	2
Kit pouches	2
Yoke	1
Carabineer and cord	1
Mosquito net	1
Waterbottle and mug	1
Aide memoir	1
Lightweight silk cover	1
Filter bag	1
Stone sharpener	1
Compass Silva	1
Magazines (M16)	5
BFA (BFA)	1
Cleaning kit (M16)	1

DON'T CHEAT

There was a time when, if a member of selection having had his rucksack weighed and found to be on the light side a brick, and in some cases several bricks, would be added. Those caught cheating would be expected to carry this extra weight for the remaining duration of the route. This practice, however, has improved, instead of bricks they are now given more useful items such as extra food or clothing.

Forget about getting a mate to transport you around in his car, dropping you just a few kilometres from the RV. You will get caught, and this means instant RTU.

LOST PROCEDURE

It is extremely unlikely that you will get lost during selection, either as an individual or as part of a group. However, serious survival conditions can arise in the Brecon Beacons in winter and have caused many student deaths. It is therefore wise to be prepared for any eventuality. To aid the student in such circumstances, all will have the proper survival equipment in their bergens. The bergens will also have a large red panel on them that will help to locate the student if the need for a rescue should arise.

You will be instructed fully on lost procedures currently in force, and these instructions should be followed without question. The lost procedures will be put into motion by any student still unaccounted for at the end of the day. If you happen to get lost, stay calm and be assured that you will be looked for. In the mean time, concentrate on staying alive and take precautions against hypothermia.

The SAS training squadron will normally start a search from the approximate position that the student was last seen. Due to their special knowledge of the Brecon Beacons in general and the selection routes in particular, the SAS usually find the missing student quickly. However, if this does not happen, or if adverse weather prevents a quick search, then the

Brecon Mountain Rescue Team, call sign Zebra, will be called in to help.

A helicopter extraction of the casualty may be used, particularly in cases of injury or hypothermia. In these cases, the helicopter will land as close as it can to the casualty. If the terrain is too rough for this, it will hover above the casualty instead and send down a winch man to help. At all times in a helicopter rescue, bear in mind that the pilot is in charge and that he has to make decisions based on certain criteria:

- Aircraft safety
- Winch man safety
- Casualty safety.

EXPOSURE

Exposure is the serious effects of climatic conditions on the body, in particular, high winds, wet and cold. The essential feature of exposure is the way in which body heat is reduced by severe chilling of the body. These conditions increase due to prolonged outdoor activity and are a combination of cold, fatigue and mental stress.

In normal conditions the inner core of our body remains at a constant 98.6°F while the outer shell can fall well below this. If the inner-core temperature starts to deviate too much either way, this can lead to mental disorientation, loss of muscular co-ordination, unconsciousness, heart failure and death. To prevent this the body will automatically restrict the blood flow to the body surface, where under exposed conditions it will be cooled. Any treatment to by-pass this, such as peripheral stimulation, alcohol, hot water or rubbing is dangerous and must be avoided.

COLD

Cold is one of the greatest enemies of survival and one that you will come across during SAS selection. It not only damages the body, it also numbs the mind. Its insidious effects weaken the will and take away the ability to think clearly. It needs to be recognized and guarded against before it takes hold.

FATIGUE

Fatigue can be an extremely debilitating and unexpected source of danger. It can sap away your will so that you don't care about what will or will not happen to you. You may then begin to neglect your safety.

Fatigue can arise from many different sources, not all of them physical. Boredom, dissatisfaction, a lack of hope or any real goal can all lead to fatigue. In some ways, fatigue becomes a way of escape out of a situation that may feel overwhelming. However, if the fatigue and its sources can be recognized and resisted, unknown reserves of strength can often be found and drawn upon.

FROSTBITE AND HYPOTHERMIA

Frostbite and hypothermia can occur after exposure to temperatures below freezing, especially in wet and/or windy conditions. The risk of frostbite and hypothermia increases in windy conditions because the wind has the effect of decreasing air temperature. This is known as a wind-chill factor. For example, air having a temperature of −20°C and moving at 48 k.p.h. (30 m.p.h.) will have the same chill factor as air with a temperature of −40°C moving only at 8 k.p.h. (5 m.p.h.). If conditions are wet as well as cold, this increases the danger because body heat can be leached away by the cold, wet air.

Take special care of hands and feet, because they are at the extremities of our circulation and lose heat rapidly. Great care must be taken to keep them warm and under cover as much as possible. When necessary, hands may be warmed under armpits or between the thighs. Frost-nipped toes can be warmed against a companion, or by moving the feet, wriggling and rubbing them. Fastenings at the ankles, wrists, neck and waist need to be efficient but not so tight as to restrict blood flow.

Frostbite

Frostbite can often occur before you become aware of it and is a very serious condition. Early symptoms of the affected part include the sensation of pins and needles, tingling, stiffness and numbness, although not all of these are necessarily present at the same time. Later, the skin affected by the frostbite will become greyish or whitish in colour. If untreated, gangrene may then develop, leading to the death of that part.

Any areas of exposed skin, especially around the face and nose, should be checked frequently and any areas of suspected frostbite should be slowly and naturally warmed. The best method is skin to skin, for example hands in armpits, but warm water could also be used as long as the temperature is checked first. To do this, dip your elbow into the water − if it is comfortable for your elbow, then the temperature is all right. The casualty also needs to be insulated against any further body-heat loss by the addition of extra blankets and/or clothing. Provide some shelter as soon as you can and, if possible, give some hot food and drink. If frostbite is detected:

- DO NOT rub or massage the affected area.
- DO NOT apply snow or ice. This is dangerous.
- DO NOT expose the affected part to a fire or use hot stones.
- DO NOT let the casualty drink alcohol.
- DO NOT let the casualty walk on a recently frost-bitten foot.
- DO NOT break open any blisters which may appear.

Hypothermia

Hypothermia occurs when body heat is lost more quickly than it can be replaced. Cold wet weather, wet clothing, immersion in cold water, exhaustion, inadequate clothing and lack of food and drink can all increase the risk of hypothermia. It is difficult to diagnose in its early stages, so extra vigilance must be ensured, especially if subject to any of the above conditions. Symptoms of hypothermia include:

- Paleness and severe, uncontrollable shivering.
- Being unusually cold to the touch.
- Fatigue and muscular weakness.
- Drowsiness and dimming of sight.
- Faint heartbeat and shallow breathing.
- Eventual collapse and unconsciousness which may lead to death.

The personality of someone suffering from hypothermia may also change, for example, a normally quiet person may become aggressive. Hypothermia must be treated as death can occur rapidly. Treatment consists of stopping the loss of heat from the body and then slowly replacing the warmth already lost, as is detailed below.

- Shelter against the cold and wind must be provided as soon as possible.
- Replace any wet clothing with dry clothing and/or coverings where possible. Do this by replacing the wet clothing a bit at a time, so that only small sections of the body are uncovered at any one time, and then only for a short while.
- When dry clothing is not available, leave the casualty in the wet garments, but provide as much extra insulation against the cold as is practicable. Finally, add a waterproof layer. An excellent object for this purpose is a metallized emergency blanket. It is windproof, waterproof and reflects radiated body heat.
- Provide body warmth – either from another healthy survivor, or, if the casualty is conscious, give him hot food and drink.

If hypothermia is encountered, remember, there are two other actions to take:

- Even if you cannot detect breathing or a heartbeat, proceed with treatment, using assisted breathing and chest compressions if necessary. Do not assume that the casualty is dead unless he still does not revive after a normal body temperature has been reached.
- The casualty must be handled carefully, as frozen skin and flesh are damaged very easily.

DEALING WITH HEAT EXHAUSTION

It is also possible for selection students to suffer from heat exhaustion. This is normally caused by excessive sweating due to the hot weather and arduous routes. The simple answer is to rest in the shade, cooling the head with a water-drenched cloth while replenishing your body fluids with small mouthfuls of water. Of secondary importance to water is *salt*. The normal human requires 10 grams each day to maintain a healthy balance. Sweat contains salt as well as water, and this loss must be replaced. If it is not then you will suffer from heatstroke, heat exhaustion and muscular cramps. The signs of salt deficiency are sudden weakness and a hot dry sensation to the body. Resting and a small pinch of salt added to a mug of water will eliminate these feelings very quickly. In dry desert or sweaty jungle conditions it is advisable to add a small amount of salt to *all* your fluid intake.

SURVIVAL SHELTERS

If you do become lost, injured, or trapped by the weather you will be advised to build some form of survival shelter. After you have assessed your situation, decide upon your survival priorities, especially where shelter is concerned. A survival situation on the Brecon Beacons in winter might make shelter an extremely urgent priority. It is important to protect yourself against the factors that can induce hypothermia: cold, wind, rain and snow. Remember, if you are lost, cold and wet, *get out of the wind*.

Blankets, canvas, sacks, plastic sheeting and ground sheets can all be used to make a shelter. Foliage, when available, can be used. If there are no trees and plants around, consider turf blocks or rocks and stones. With a bit of improvisation, the wind chill factor can always be reduced.

FORESTS AND WOODS

Large fallen logs can be found in any forest area. If two such logs are placed close together, a trough can be dug between them, and, without much effort, a roof constructed of branches and foliage. Even if you only have one log available, you can improvise by building a low earth wall, or it can be used as the basis of a small lean-to.

The Lean-To

The lean-to frame, made of an interwoven lattice work of twigs and branches, is simple to construct and is considered the most basic of shelters. The lean-to frame can be covered by almost anything: a ground sheet; foliage; plastic sacks; wreckage panels, and even turf. In fact, turf or a layer of mud on top of foliage makes it wind and waterproof and stops the shelter from being blown away. Remember though, when building the lean-to, always point the down slope of the roof into the prevailing wind. The sides of the lean-to can also be filled in – turf blocks or foliage and mud again being the best materials.

Layered Tree Bivouac

Any small tree can provide the means of constructing this type of small shelter. Find a point on the trunk at about shoulder height and partially cut through it. Then, leaving the stem attached to the butt, push the upper portion over until its top rests on the ground. Cut off the branches on the underside of the trunk. The upstanding branches on the outside can then be broken so that they hang down. This basic frame can now be thatched using the foliage taken from the underside.

PLAINS AND GRASSLANDS

You may need to make a shelter on grassland where there are few trees. A shelter may still be constructed from turf bricks. It can be roofed with turf or, if available, any kind of sheeting (anchored by the top turf blocks). Branches and boughs form the easiest support for a turf roof. If these can't be found, the shelter will have to be built smaller and the sods for the roof will have to be cut longer. They can then be used in pairs to support each other. Make sure that if it rains, the rain will drain away from the trench and not into it.

If you find yourself surviving in conditions where heat is a problem, then going below ground is the best answer. Bear in mind that this may be difficult if the ground is hard. In cold conditions, the addition of a fire and fire reflector improve the comfort of all shelters, especially lean-to varieties. Green logs and sticks are best for building both the base of the fire, and the interwoven fire reflector. Large stones can also be used to reflect heat; these are stacked up around the back of the fire. At night, these same stones can be taken from their position and carefully placed beneath your sleeping space where they will give out their warmth all night.

SNOW SHELTERS

There can be up to three feet of snow on the Brecon Beacons during February and early March; therefore you may need to build a shelter in an emergency. There are several different types of snow shelter, but some are unsuitable for the limited time and energy of a solitary survivor. Below are two examples that can be easily constructed:

The Snow Trench

As an emergency measure, even a hole in the snow can be used as a simple temporary shelter for one man. This could be improved upon by a roof – of snow if it is hard enough, or of branches or sheeting if it is not.

The Fir-Tree Snow Shelter

Large fir trees can be used as the basis of a simple snow shelter. Dig the snow away from the base of the tree trunk, and pile it up on either side of your shelter to improve protection. You will probably find that there is already a natural hollow in the snow at the base so this will help to get you started. Then, on the side furthest from your shelter, cut the tree's lower branches for use either as bedding material, or to weave into the branches overhanging the shelter for better overhead protection. If you wish to build a fire, build one some way around the trunk from your shelter to avoid the heat melting the snow in the branches above it.

SUMMARY

The first part of selection is by far the most difficult. To have any chance you must focus your mind on doing everything well. Don't fall in with the boozers who will want to go drinking every night – they will soon be gone. Keep your own counsel until the field has dwindled down to around thirty students or so. Don't pester the DS, and listen to their advice. They are not there to trip you up.

The first few weeks are vital. Always keep in mind why you came to Hereford in the first place and give it your all.

CHAPTER FOUR

Continuation Training

Once the candidate has passed selection, he will go on to continuation training. This is where he will learn and hone all the necessary skills required of an SAS soldier. The basics of weapon training, patrolling skills, and Standard Operational Procedures (SOPs) are taught, as well as taking part in escape and evasion exercises, parachuting and finally, five weeks jungle training. To enter a squadron it is necessary to be able to swim and dive. If a candidate cannot do either, he will be put on a crash course to learn them. On acceptance, he will receive the beige beret with its famed winged dagger. This is a very special moment, and a fantastic feeling, as anyone in the SAS will tell you.

DRESS

Continuation training is more teaching-based than test-based, so by this stage you should be getting a better idea of how the SAS think and act during the outdoor exercises. You should also start considering the way the SAS dress. During combat situations, the normal dress is an SAS windproof smock, windproof trousers and a woollen hat or cap. A Norwegian shirt is usually worn underneath the smock, as well as other layers, depending on the climate. Your equipment can be divided into two parts: belt kit and bergen. Items contained in the SAS belt kit include: magazines for immediate use, water, a medic pack and an E & E (Escape and Evasion) kit. The latter should be carried at all times as it contains essential survival items that will enable a soldier to make it back to his own lines (see Survival Training). Belt kits may also contain search and rescue beacons. Bergens contain everything else the soldier needs, such as his sleeping bag and sleeping mat, water rations, secondary ammunition and explosives. In a bug-out situation after a hard contact with the enemy, bergens are mostly abandoned and the soldier will escape with only his belt kit. The exception to this is the signaller who will also take his radio set. This is always carried in a separate bag on top of the bergen so that it can be grabbed easily.

WEAPONS USED BY THE SAS

The first thing to remember about any weapon is safety. Standard Operating Procedures, or SOPs are designed to prevent mishaps and have been developed over many years. The Regiment has few rules set in stone, but these SOPs are. They control the way the SAS behaves on an operation, especially during patrols. Basically, SOPs are a list of rules, 'dos and don'ts', that need to be learned and followed. If you do this, you will be more likely to stay out of trouble. An important SOP where weapons are concerned is to always perform a safety check when you put down or pick up a weapon. Do this even if the person that passed you the weapon has just performed the same check. Remember this, it will save you a lot of trouble.

During continuation, you will receive training on a wide array of weapons, both British and foreign. The SAS soldier may find himself in combat situations where he will need to be proficient with any type of weapon. A typical example of this was in Mirbat where the SAS attachment fired SLRs, AR15s, .50 Brownings, GPMGs, 81mm Mortar, and a 25-pound artillery gun. I personally trained with and fired over fifty different types of weapon during my time with the Regiment, and that doesn't include the ones I have forgotten about. Here is a brief description of some of the weapons you will encounter.

SA80

Most soldiers on SAS selection will have basic infantry skills and will be familiar with the SA80, the standard personal weapon in use with the British Army. However, the Regiment dislikes the SA80 and has tended to use the American M16. The Regiment will expect you to become acquainted with and proficient in the use of normal infantry weapons, both personal and support. These will include the SIG Sauer P226, GPMG, 81mm mortar, etc.

M16/203

The M16, with a 203 grenade launcher clipped underneath is the preferred weapon of any SAS soldier operating in combat mode. Despite challenges from other, newer types of weapon, the M16 has remained a firm favourite within the Regiment. There are many reasons for this: it is reliable, able to operate in all conditions; it is accurate and suitable both for close range work in the jungle as well as the wider open spaces of the desert. It is light as is the ammunition and with a 30-round magazine, it keeps up a good fire pattern, and can be fitted with a simple bipod that clips to the barrel.

Right: Many of the volunteers who took part in the series were not used to carrying a rifle. They were made to have it within arm's length at all times, even when sleeping or going to the toilet.

Below: From time to time our volunteers received a little 'beasting' – that's military jargon for being run ragged. Here they are made to run the off-road vehicle course.

Left: Walking up and running down hills is the only way to get good timings on SAS selection.

Bottom left: Three times up and down Ben Lomond with a 35lb bergen was a little bit too much for some of our volunteers. Totally exhausted, Jason McKinlay collapses halfway through the Point to Point exercise.

Below: Good map reading is a must for both our volunteers and the SAS. Cassius Frankson struggled to come to terms with it which cost him time and distance.

Presenter Dermot O'Leary talks to Jason McKinlay halfway through Long Drag. The route covers 40 miles and the volunteers have to carry a 55lb bergan plus a rifle. It is this kind of exercise which highlights the difference between civilian and military fitness.

Those that managed to complete the first three days were dressed in old First World War greatcoats ready for combat survival – few knew what was to come. With nothing more than a button compass and a sketch map with which to navigate, they were sent to walk in appalling weather conditions.

Left: At the end of Long Drag and 24 hours without sleep the exhausted volunteers are expected to swim the loch. Their clothes are placed in their bergen which is then waterproofed by a black plastic bin bag. The bag serves as a flotation aid on which the volunteer's rifle is placed as they swim.

Left: Those volunteers who were captured were hooded and taken to the interrogation centre. Here they were made to stand in the stress position: a position they were made to hold for up to four hours at a time. White sound and intimidation techniques broke down their resolve not to talk.

Above left: A volunteer is taken for a medical check-up after completing the interrogation exercise. Although confronted by a friendly, familiar face many could not believe it was over.

Above right: The remaining volunteers were all given a hot meal and a good night's rest – they would need both.

Below: Professional parachute instructors take over the day's training. A few hours later and the first volunteer was jumping from an aircraft at 12,000 feet. It was an experience – but not for the fainthearted.

Left: Colin Hill lands safely on the ground after his first parachute jump.

Below: Patrol 2 plan their mission during the Target Recce exercise.

Above left: The handling of and firing of foreign weapons is very much in keeping with SAS selection skills. Gary Robertson prepares to enter the jungle shooting range.

Above right: The volunteers find out what it's like to operate in a respirator.

Below: With camouflage paint applied, Colin Hill checks his weapons prior to the final assault.

Staff Sergeant Eddie Stone briefs the remaining volunteers for the Target Recce exercise.

Two of the finalists, Gary Robertson (left) and Colin Hill relax in the base camp.

Field Stripping M16

Clear the rifle and make it safe. To avoid accidental firing, always look into the chamber after clearing the weapon to make sure it does not contain a round.

1. Place selector lever to safe (this can only be done when the weapon is cocked).
2. Remove the magazine by depressing the magazine catch, and pull the magazine forward.
3. Lock the bolt open by pulling the cocking handle to the rear and engaging the bolt catch.
4. Ensure that the selector is at safe and check in the chamber to make sure that it contains no ammunition. With the selector still at safe, press the upper half of the bolt catch allowing the bolt to go forward.
5. Place the selector to SEMI and squeeze the trigger to release the tension on the hammer spring.

Stripping

1. Remove the sling if attached.
2. Stand the weapon butt upright on a firm surface and depress the slip ring at the chamber end of the hand guard.
3. Remove both sections of the hand guard from the slip ring and pull down to unclip from the foresight sleeve.
4. Use a round to push out the two takedown pins located at the rear of the selector and the front of the magazine housing to separate the weapon.
5. Pull back the charging handle assembly to remove the bolt carrier assembly.
6. Remove the charging handle by pulling back and down.
7. Move bolt assembly forward to unlocking position and remove firing pin retaining pin. Do not open or close the split end of the firing pin retaining pin.

8. Push in the bolt assembly to put in the locked position.
9. Catch firing pin as it drops out of the rear of the bolt carrier assembly.
10. Give the square cam pin a quarter turn and lift out.
11. Remove bolt assembly from the bolt carrier assembly.

It is possible to strip the weapon further by removing the extractor and spring assembly. The buffer spring can be removed from the butt, but this is not normally done during daily stripping. Reassembly is a straight reversal of the stripping steps.

SIG Sauer P226

This pistol is made by one of the oldest Swiss weapons manufacturers, SIG (Schweizerische Industrie Gesellschaft), which was founded back in the 1800s. SIGs weapons have always had a reputation for being expensive, but that is because they have such an excellent record for accuracy, mainly attributed to the length of the bearing surfaces between the slide and the frame. In the early 1960s SIG entered the international market with a new range of pistols by-passing Swiss arms export laws by making a marketing agreement with a German company. The SIG Sauer P226, with its 15-round magazine, has now largely replaced the Browning High-Power within the SAS.

HK MP5

Heckler and Koch produce some of the finest machine-guns in the world, and they have become an icon in the battle against terrorism. The company was founded in 1947 by three former employees of Mauser. To begin with, they did not make weapons, but by 1959, they returned to their original trade and had their first commercial success when their G3 assault rifle was adopted by the West German army. The MP5 developed from the G3 and shares many of its characteristics, especially its relatively light weight. It was first used by German border police, but can now be seen slung around the necks of any half-decent anti-terrorist team. In fact, it can almost be read as a symbol of the men who fight against terrorism, just as the AK47 has come to symbolize those that cause it.

Most Heckler and Koch weapons are variations of one model and this makes most parts interchangeable between models. The stripping and assembly of most models in the range is much the same – for example, the three-pin system is similar in most models, including the infantry weapons and sniper rifles. This makes learning the safety aspects of the range a little easier for the SAS soldier. Once the theory has been learned, the soldier then moves on to the firing range, where, as with the pistol, he will start off with the basics before progressing on to more advanced techniques. This will involve such exercises as combination shooting with both the MP5 and the SIG, slowly progressing to working with a partner taking on multiple targets. The SAS soldier will have the opportunity to try out all the different models of pistol and MP5.

Firing Heckler and Koch Sub-Machine Guns

- Take hold of the weapon, right hand on the pistol grip, left hand on the forward handgrip.
- Use the thumb of your right hand to set the selector to safe.
- Pull the cocking handle to the rear with your left hand and hook it into the retaining notch.
- Insert a full magazine into the housing and clip it home.
- Use your left hand in a chopping motion to release the cocking handle.

- Use the right thumb to change the selector to single shot or automatic.
- Aim and fire.
- When the magazine is empty, the working parts will stay closed. Repeat the process.

AK

Most soldiers have heard of the old Soviet Kalashnikov, the standard infantry weapon of many communist regimes. In many poorer countries, it is a popular weapon because it is relatively cheap, extremely robust and will operate under almost any conditions. All the AKs I have seen, both originals and copies, have been good weapons.

The AK47 is the older version, and fires a 7.62mm round as does the later AKM. However, the latest version, the AK74, fires a 5.45mm round. Despite the alterations that the AK74 has undergone, it still looks and operates as it did before. A magazine is inserted into the magazine housing and clipped into place by pulling back firmly (7.62 mags will not fit on the 5.45 weapons). The selector lever on the right side of the weapon just above the trigger is set to fire, allowing the weapon to be cocked. When the working parts are released, a round is fed into the chamber. The selector can then be set to safe, single shot or full automatic. When the magazine is empty, the chamber remains closed.

Field Stripping AK

- Remove the magazine, cock the weapon, and clear the chamber.
- Push the catch at the rear of the top cover and remove.
- Push the same catch forwards again, and rotate to remove the spring, rod and carrier.

- The bolt rotates out of the carrier.
- The gas tube is removed by turning up the latch on the right of the rear sight and lifting the tube off.

RPG7

Another weapon associated with communist forces worldwide, the RPG (Reaktiviniy Protivotankoviy Granatomet) has been in use for almost as long as the AK. It is a simple but very effective weapon, which, despite being replaced by the more accurate RPG16, will doubtless be around for some years to come.

There are two sights on the RPG: an optical one, which has an internal light for night aiming, and a flip-up, iron-battle sight. The optical sight has horizontal graded lines that give elevation on which the lead and windage corrections are marked off at ten mil intervals. This gives the sight a greater accuracy than the actual weapon, because the chances of the RPG hitting its target decrease as the range increases. Although I have tried several times, hitting an exposed target over 400 metres is just about impossible. In addition to these sights, the weapon can also be fitted with a Soviet NSP2 infra-red night sight, which can detect targets up to 200 metres away. Before it is to be fired, the warhead must first be assembled with the motor charge and any booster and then fed into the front of the weapon. When loaded, the percussion cap must be aligned with the hammer before the nose cap is removed and the safety pin taken out. According to the Russian manual, the ideal range is supposed to be 300 metres, but I suggest that to hit a target, half that distance would be better. When the hammer falls, a strip powder charge ignites the rocket, projecting it at 100 metres per second. Upon leaving the barrel, four stabilizing fins spring out, and the rocket arms itself under a ball inertia release. After about 11 metres, a booster rocket cuts in and the missile speeds up to 200 metres per second. If the missile misses its target, it will self destruct between 700 and 900 metres.

UNCOMMON WEAPONS

The SAS have to also be familiar with weapons used by the enemy or terrorists. Because of this, the Regiment has access to many different types of weapons. Other specialist weapons may be chosen for their suitability for a covert option or a silent kill – a crossbow or the MP5K briefcase model, for example. Here are just a few specialist weapons.

FN Minimi

This 5.56 calibre light machine-gun has been a standard American squad weapon (M249), since 1982. The weapon has an interesting design in that it can use either disintegrating belt links, standard M16 magazines, or a 200-round box magazine of loose belt which can be fixed directly on to the weapon. It more than proved its worth with the SAS during the Gulf War, when they found it very effective during some of their more exciting moments.

Mark 19 Grenade Thrower

This 40mm grenade launcher really needs to be mounted, as it was during the Gulf War. It has an automatic belt feed of 20 or 50 rounds, with a range of up to 1500 metres. The unusual thing about the disintegrating belt feed is that, when the cartridge is ejected, the link remains with it. This American-made weapon can field an impressive array of high explosive, anti-tank and anti-personnel grenades and is extremely useful for laying down heavy, suppressive fire.

Sniper Rifles

The SAS have used several sniper rifles over the years. The first one to be used was the old L42, a sturdy, reliable and reasonably accurate weapon, but soon surpassed by the newer, high-tech rifles. The Tikka Finlander has also been used, but the weapons currently in use are the G3 and the Accuracy International PM 7.62 Snipers Rifle. The PM is a bolt-action 7.62 rifle with a stainless-steel barrel, and will give head shots at 300–600 metres. Apart from being comfortable to fire, the head need not be removed during bolt operation thus making it easier for continuous observation. It has a bipod and there is a retractable spike on the rear of the butt. The box magazine holds twelve rounds and it is fitted with a standard Schmidt and Bender 6 × 42 telescopic sight. Another sniper rifle in use is the Heckler and Koch G3SG. This is used by the SAS for close range targets, at a distance of 200–300 metres. This self-loading rifle is basically a G3 with an up-graded barrel, a variable trigger and a comfortable butt. It is also a good weapon for multiple targets, or rapid long range shooting.

Arwen

The Arwen is a 37mm gas, smoke thrower and baton-round propeller. It has a five-round rotating magazine, which is part of the weapon and works very similar to the cylinder on an old-fashioned revolver. The baton round will do immobilizing damage up to a hundred metres, although the accuracy is not all that good. The CS gas rounds vary, some are capable of penetration, through either light wooded doors and glass, before discharging.

Winchester/Remington Shotguns

These are generally only used by the anti-terrorist teams to remove doors, etc. Both are pump-action shotguns and the most common round used is solid lead ball. However, gas and buckshot can also be used.

Stun Grenade

The SAS required a weapon that would give them vital seconds to come to grips with terrorists. The Royal Ordnance experimented with various devices and eventually came up with the stun grenade, which was deemed suitable. It consists of a G60, which makes a loud noise (160 dB), combined with a high light output (300,000cd) without producing any harmful fragmentation. The effect is a bit like a flashing strobe in a disco but a million times stronger. Anyone in close proximity to a stun grenade when it goes off will be stunned and unable to move for about 3–5 seconds, which makes it a very useful item in the anti-terrorism armoury.

RANGE WORK

SAS operations require that the soldier be proficient with many basic weapons. The weapons training normally starts off with pistol handling, and, irrespective of the weapon used, the basic procedures are always the same. Safety is the first priority, followed by stripping and assembly, then on to basic shooting. At first, the soldier will shoot facing the target, but as he develops his skills, he will learn to shoot from different positions, and will eventually learn to engage more than one target at the same time.

Practice is the key to good responsive shooting, and at

Hereford it is positively encouraged: the Regiment's expenditure on ammunition is very high. As well as the many ranges, exercises take place in the famous 'Killing House', or Close Quarter Battle building. Here, the members of the SAS anti-terrorist team spend hundreds of hours training and perfecting their individual shooting skills. The structure was designed with this in mind and allows for training in many different sets of circumstances.

One well-known technique that is learned here is the SAS 'double-tap' – firing two shots in rapid succession. This is not an easy skill to learn and it may take years to feel comfortable with this method. However, in action, the 'double-tap' has proved itself over and over again. It is good to remember that two rounds will stop a terrorist far better than one. Once the pistol is mastered, the student then moves on to the more advanced techniques using automatic weaponry.

Another necessary skill practised in the 'Killing House' is the hostage snatch. VIPs tend to be potential targets for kidnapping by terrorists, and so many are keen to visit the Hereford base to view the anti-terrorist team in action. This can often be an advantage to the Regiment for it gives them the chance to practice with a 'real' hostage, as it were. Even without the VIP, the team would be training; unless on exercise or an operation, they are permanently based in the camp.

The VIPs that volunteer to be hostages find themselves in the complete darkness and absolute silence of the 'Killing House', wondering whatever possessed them to do this in the first place. All of a sudden, the door bursts open and a stun grenade detonates just inches away. Laser beams search for targets as live rounds of ammunition fly around them. At this stage the VIPs do not move: not because that is what they have been to told to do, or even that they may be hit by a bullet. Their lack of movement is due to fear, in this situation a vital response for survival. Within moments they are picked up rather roughly and literally thrown out of the room by the black-clad figures only to discover that they have not sustained a single scratch to their persons. They will now be able to tell you what hell is like.

BUILDING AN OBSERVATION POST (OP)

One of the strengths of the SAS is the way they can get in and get out of a position without being seen. Much emphasis will be put on this skill during training as the ability to remain undetected is of vital importance, not only to yourself, but to the whole mission. The success of this kind of operation depends on two important factors: selecting a route and building a good OP. You will learn these skills during continuation training.

When approaching a target, the SAS uses much the same military formations and tactics as any normal infantry patrol. Stealth is important as the patrol will need to see and avoid the enemy in order to prevent a compromise. Success of the mission depends on the team reaching their objective un-detected. An SAS patrol usually consists of a basic unit of four men. Small numbers are able to infiltrate behind enemy lines more easily and leave less signs. Normally, these patrols consist of a signaller, a demolitions expert, a linguist and a medic, although quite often the members will have cross-trained in more than one discipline.

The lead scout is often the most experienced member of the team. This is an extremely responsible position, as the scout is the 'eyes and ears' of the patrol, detecting signs of enemy presence and anticipating the possibility of a contact. He is well trained as a tracker and can read even the smallest of tell-tale signs. He is also responsible for finding the best route for the patrol to reach its objective. Behind the scout will normally be the commander, who will be ready to cover his scout at the first sign of a contact, as well as making sure that he has the right bearings. Behind the commander come the signaller and fourth person respectively.

The pace of the patrol will depend on their exposure, for they have to be ready to face an unexpected enemy ambush at any time. The route taken may force the commander to choose between speed and concealment and the patrol will need to move faster in areas of sparse cover. On the other hand, if the vegetation is thick, the patrol will have to move slower in order to avoid making noise or bumping unexpectedly into the enemy. Silence is imperative and a set of standard military hand signals are used for communication on the move. A beta light is used to check the map during stops.

Although all these skills will be taught to you during continuation training, here are a few helpful tips to aid you.

- Never move down roads or tracks.
- Avoid areas of habitation.
- Travel by night if possible.
- Remember your basic camouflage: Shape, Shine, Shadow, Silhouette, Smell, Sound, and Movement.
- Restrict all eating until you have stopped. Cook before it gets too dark.
- When you overnight somewhere, clear the area. Have a single approach route and escape route.
- Loop your own approach route so that you can observe it. The enemy may have picked up your trail.
- Keep your weapon to hand at all times. If you move, so does it.
- Anything you are not using goes back into the bergen.
- In enemy territory, sleep in full gear, including your boots.
- Try to avoid smoking; cigarettes give off light and they stink.

- Avoid using soap or perfumed products; in damp air they can be smelt for several hundred metres.

THE HIDE

Being concealed from the enemy can sometimes be a short affair, but can sometimes last for several weeks. No matter the length of time, the important factors are to not be seen, heard or smelt. Your place of concealment may be in a building, and if that building is occupied, then you are going to have to be extremely quiet. Without going into too much detail, it is quite simple to get into a building. The Regiment will teach you the skill of lock-picking, which can take many years to master despite being simple in theory. Other methods of entry are by removing doors, getting on to roofs and through sky-lights. The hard part is to remain undetected when you get inside. The bodily needs of sleeping, eating and going to the toilet, as well as having to change places with your partner can prove to be quite a challenge.

How long an urban OP will go on for depends on how many men you can get into the hide, and how often it can be re-supplied. I once spent three weeks in the cramped loft of a town hall where there was just enough room for one man to lie down and the other to sit taking photographs. Each man would spend four hours on watch and four sleeping. We were re-supplied every third night, lowering our waste and exposed film down a line and exchanging it for food and other supplies. Despite the town hall being occupied both night and day, we managed to remain undetected and collect enough comprom-ising photographs of our suspect to later persuade him to provide us with information.

If your hide is in the countryside, then it may be possible to use natural camouflage. If not, a hide may be constructed that makes the most of the natural resources around. In some circumstances, such as arctic conditions, one may be formed out of natural and artificial substances. The ideal site for a hide will be one where you are able to remain concealed and yet be able to observe your target at the same time. This is not always possible and it may be necessary to move a small distance from the hide in order to make the observations. Once the hide is established, self-discipline is vital. Sloppiness will lead the enemy to see signs of your presence.

During the Falklands Conflict, members of G Squadron set up hides in order to observe Argentine positions. These hides often took the shape of small caves and rocky outcrops in which they remained, in appalling circumstances, for up to three weeks (prior to the main force coming ashore). They had to remain motionless by day in clothing that was totally inadequate for the conditions – it was several weeks before the Gore-Tex clothing arrived. In order to signal base, the patrols had to move away from their hide each night, often covering a round distance of twenty miles, so that the Argentines would not be able to monitor them. They were not able to cook either, due to their close proximity to the enemy, so this denied them the only source of warmth available. They coped because they were self-disciplined.

In the Gulf War concealment also played its part, albeit in a slightly different manner. The fighting columns sent behind enemy lines were forced to hide their vehicles during daylight hours, a difficult task considering their proximity to Baghdad and the fact that they were surrounded by the enemy. The vehicles were camouflaged to blend in with the terrain, and the column would form a loose circle, normally in a shallow depression. This gave cover from line of sight, and allowed them to place sentries on high ground. For the whole six weeks that the columns were in Iraq, they remained undetected, apart from one incident when an Iraqi jeep entered the LUP and was quickly dispatched. This sort of concealment took tremendous effort and was immensely successful.

OBSERVATION EQUIPMENT

There is little point in locating and constructing a good hide if you do not have the equipment to observe the target. To this end the equipment is provided to meet the requirement, allowing the SAS soldiers to do their job properly. And while the 'mark one' eyeball is still the best, a full range of monoculars, binoculars, telescopes and periscopes can also be supplied for use in stand-off visual surveillance tasks. These are available in different sizes and varying powers of magnification according to requirements.

Night Vision Systems

A range of second Generation Plus image intensifiers, in the form of individual weapon sights (IWS), night observation devices (NODs) and night vision goggles (NVGs) are available for use during the surveillance and assault phases of all operations. NODs can be supplied in a number of sizes ranging from miniature 'pocketscopes' to large tripod-mounted models.

Infra-Red Laser Projectors

Infra-red laser projectors are available for mounting co-axially on a variety of small arms. Used in conjunction with NVGs, these enable users to project otherwise invisible aiming marks on to targets and thus engage them with maximum speed and accuracy.

Thermal Imagers

Thermal imagers can also be supplied for surveillance and target acquisition during night and day. A number of different models, varying in size from hand-held types to tripod-mounted devices co-axially mounted with laser rangefinders, are available.

A perfect example of all the patrol skills being used to achieve a successful result was the ambush by the SAS at Loughall in Northern Ireland. This involved weeks of preparation by several patrols working together, collecting information, night recces, observation and finally the ambush.

LOUGHALL

The scene of a successful ambush operation by the SAS against the Irish Republican Army (IRA). Between late 1986 and early 1987 IRA actions against the security forces had increased, especially attacks on police stations. In one of these, a mechanical digger with a bomb in its bucket damaged a Royal Ulster Constabulary (RUC) station in County Armagh. Because of these attacks, surveillance on known terrorists and suspects was increased in Northern Ireland and the security forces were placed on high alert.

In April 1987, in East Tyrone, another digger was stolen and later found on an abandoned farm 16 kilometres from Loughall. Immediately suspicions were aroused about another forthcoming police-station attack and so the farm was placed under surveillance by the RUC's E4A unit. From their hide they saw explosives being taken to the farm, so they knew their suspicions had been correct. By a stroke of luck, a short time later an IRA phone call was intercepted giving the day and time of the attack. With the nearest most likely target being Loughall police station, all the pieces were now in place for the RUC and the SAS to stage a box-type ambush on the terrorists.

On the day, RUC snipers and some SAS soldiers were placed in the empty police station while other SAS troops were placed strategically in the surrounding area. One team was positioned in the playing fields opposite the building with a general purpose machine gun.

Sure enough, the digger, with the bomb loaded in the bucket soon appeared, the driver flanked by two armed guards. Not long after, a blue Toyota van, stolen earlier in the day, also turned up. The van carried the other five members of the attack group. At 7.20 p.m., after several fake passes, the JCB crashed through the station's perimeter fence with the bomb's fuse already lit. The men in the van jumped out and sprayed the station with bullets as the three men in the digger made a run for the van. Simultaneously, the SAS and RUC opened fire on the terrorists, killing all eight. At the same moment the bomb exploded, badly damaging the building but only causing some minor injuries.

Unfortunately the incident also saw the death of one innocent civilian and the wounding of another. A white Citroën car entered the operational area, unaware of what was in process. The men inside, two brothers, were wearing the same type of blue-boiler suits as the terrorists. The SAS, thinking that the men were also part of the IRA gang, opened fire, killing the driver, Anthony Hughes.

Despite this tragedy, Loughall was seen as an extremely successful SAS operation. Eight top IRA terrorists had been taken out – a devastating blow to the terrorist organization's morale.

CHAPTER FIVE

Survival Training

Survival training is a very serious matter in the SAS. Many SAS operations involve actions behind enemy lines or in remote unfamiliar terrain where the risk of capture and the need to survive are ever present. Survival training is a fascinating subject and a wide range of experts are employed to teach the students the skills and knowledge involved. The elements of escape, evasion and survival could easily fill many books by themselves, but unfortunately here we only have a chapter in which to cover the basics.

A survival situation is one that can be defined as being unexpected, unplanned and with no obvious or immediate solution. In extreme cases, or if captured, your life could be in danger.

For a soldier, becoming a prisoner of war (POW), is a frightening ordeal. He suddenly finds that his future is uncertain, and the threats of physical violence, torture, or even death can have great psychological effects. He may feel that he is entirely alone, or even that he has been abandoned by his own side.

Despite international laws such as the Geneva Convention there are no guarantees that a prisoner of war will be treated in a humanitarian fashion. Quite often it depends upon the individual personalities and professionalism of the captors. If the captured soldier is one of a large number of POWs, the likelihood of him being singled out for harsh treatment decreases. If he is on his own it is likely that he will receive some form of beating, because he is perceived as the enemy. Local militias may be more brutal and ruthless in their treatment of POWs than professional soldiers.

Many factors can affect the amount of hostility dealt out to a newly captured POW. To their captors he is their representative of the enemy, a scapegoat for their friends, and maybe any civilians that have been killed in, for example, a bombing raid. They may have heard of alleged atrocities carried out by the enemy, or they may be losing the war. Whether their reasons are based on the truth or not, their personal perceptions and their anger can make this a dangerous time for a POW.

A POW, or a soldier in a survival situation, must also be aware of his other adversaries: pain, fatigue, boredom and loneliness. These factors may affect him psychologically, making him fearful and weak. They must be recognized and controlled before they begin to work on the mind. In taking command of these, the soldier also takes command of his situation.

DEALING WITH PAIN AND FEAR

Pain is a natural signal from your body that something is wrong. Unfortunately, even when you have recognized this fact, the pain doesn't switch off. Allowing yourself to become preoccupied with pain could lessen your chances of survival. If you can focus your mind on planning and doing things to help you survive, the pain can be lived with to a greater extent.

Fear, on the other hand, is a useful emotion. It is a normal and instinctive reaction to a threat to one's self and the possibility of actual injury, torture, or death. Fear and how we react to it can influence our ability to survive. Fear can even be beneficial in a threatening situation as it releases chemicals into the body which prepares it to deal with that situation. Denial of fear, or fear of fear, may actually put you at a disadvantage in a survival situation, because you will not be recognizing and reacting properly to dangers. Once you can accept and freely admit to fear, you will always be able to act to improve your predicament. *Never give up hope.*

ADVANTAGES OF AN EARLY ESCAPE

Remember, it is every soldier's duty to effect escape at the first opportunity. Of course, if a soldier is captured close to his own lines, his chances of a successful escape will be higher. Unless wounded or injured, he will still be fit and he may still have some of his equipment. He might also have an idea of the position of his own troops.

However, it is not advisable to attempt escape when close to the front line of a battle unless you are extremely sure of success. The tension amongst the combat troops in this position makes it more likely that you will be shot during an escape attempt.

A good opportunity for escape may present itself during transit deeper into enemy territory. Transportation may take the form of a vehicle, by foot, an aeroplane, train or boat; escape is possible from all of these. It is important to stay alert to the possibilities that may present themselves: guards may fall asleep or a diversion may be created through an air strike by friendly forces. Be an opportunist. Even if the chance to escape does not present itself, you can always try and collect any bits and pieces that might come in useful for a later attempt.

It is important to keep occupied; boredom and isolation weaken the will. Often the POW will have his hopes raised,

SAS - ARE YOU TOUGH ENOUGH?

only to see them come to nothing, or he will be forced to spend long lonely hours with nothing happening, sometimes in darkness. During times such as these the insidious effects of boredom and loneliness begin to take root. Recognize this danger and guard against it by keeping your mind active. Plan how you are going to escape, plan your future after you've escaped; talk – even if it is only to yourself. Boredom can't survive if you are thinking and acting positively.

> **SAS Tip:** during an escape and evasion exercise in Canada, I found myself separated from the rest of my troop. Carrying out the SOPs, I eventually reached the ERV (Emergency Rendezvous) and waited. When no one showed up, after the allotted time, I decided to head for the troop RV and set off across the heavily wooded wilderness. The journey took four days, and throughout the whole time I was completely by myself – no other human being within sight or sound. The experience was daunting at first, with unfamiliar noises coming out of the cold and windy forest. By the next day I began to play a game, pretending that I was a mad Canadian trapper – quite happy to be wandering alone in the wilderness. I built shelters that shielded me from the wind and I trapped two wild pheasants. By the fourth day, I found my troop again, and when I looked back upon my little adventure, I found that it had been a happy and fulfilling journey in its own right.

The following section is intended to show the range of escape possibilities available to any future POW. Although not a comprehensive guide, it will act as an inspiration to some positive thinking on the behalf of the POW.

Prisoners are nearly always confined in one or more type of structure. To escape, you have to decide whether you want to go under, over or through. Then you have to work out how to do it. Analysing the structure of your prison will give you the answer.

Examine the floor, walls and ceiling thoroughly. Take notice of any plumbing or electrical features. If you are taken away from your cell, try to observe your immediate surroundings. Note the guards' routines, mealtimes, etc. Think of the information as another tool; then begin to plan your means of escape.

WALLS

There are five basic types of wall: brick, block, stone, reenforced concrete and timber. Most of these structures present an opportunity for escape.

Brick

Brick walls are the most common type of wall that a POW will encounter. The strength of the brick wall is its bond. Once this has been broken, it is a fairly easy matter to get through it.

To do this, first select your exit point, preferably a place that is hidden by some other object, e.g. a bed. Start at the middle with one brick and scrape away all the mortar around it using an improvised chisel. This may take several days as the first brick is always the hardest. Make sure that there is no likelihood of your being heard or disturbed by the guards.

To prevent your work from being discovered, gather up the mortar dust at the end of each session and mix it to a paste with a little liquid – water or urine will do. If you are able to add soap, this will improve the binding even more. Use this mortar paste to refill the gaps, when you replace the bricks. The bond in the wall will have been broken after the removal of the first brick, however several bricks may have to be removed in this way before the rest are loose enough to be wrenched out by hand.

Blocks

Many modern buildings are constructed from large concrete blocks. Although larger, and more difficult to remove in one piece, they should be treated in the same manner as bricks. Many blocks are hollow inside, and this makes them easier to break. If an improvised hammer and chisel are available, a single thickness of wall can be smashed through quite quickly. For this purpose, a short piece of steel pipe, maybe from some plumbing facilities in your cell, would make a good sledgehammer. Note, though, that noise may be a limiting factor in this method of escape.

Stone

Older buildings are often built with thick walls of stone. This can make escape through difficult, but not impossible. The bond-breaking method can be used, although due to the different sizes and shapes of the stones, it will take much longer. It is advisable, therefore, to check for other means of escape such as windows and doors. In an older building these are often in a dilapidated and weakened state and may be broken through in order to effect an escape.

Timber

Timber buildings are fairly easy to break out of, unless they are constructed out of solid logs. If a piece of metal piping is available, flatten one end and use it to force apart overlapping panels. A good escape hole can be made if the nails are removed from the panels. Escape via the roof forms another possibility, as does escape via the floor. Many wooden huts, being temporary structures, are placed upon earth foundations that may be tunnelled through.

Re-enforced Concrete

Escape from a re-enforced concrete building is more problematical. Luckily, this material is usually only used on foundations and special buildings. Don't try to escape through the walls as this is next to impossible. Instead, try to find another way out, such as through a window, door, air vent or sewer.

FENCES

Fences are not usually used as a permanent form of confinement for POWs. They will be found either as temporary enclosures or as a secondary perimeter barrier. Fence types vary greatly in the way they are made, the thickness of the wire, and the wire type. These factors need to be studied if it is planned to break through a fence.

How a fence is constructed and manufactured will determine the method of escape. For example, some fence sections can be collapsed just by cutting the correct pattern of links. In other cases, the wire may be too thick to cut through and the fence is best climbed. In this instance, the POW must be sure that the fence will bear his weight.

Some wires are designed to cause injury, for example, razor wire. If the sacking POW decides to climb a fence with such wire, he must ensure that he is protected by some padding.

In summary, the principle is the same for fences as it is with walls: study, plan and decide whether to go over, under or through.

Links

Interwoven metal links form the basis of most fences. Knowing how to cut the links in a set pattern will save time and energy when escaping. Some modern prisons have a solid mesh metal fence and these are better climbed than cut. This can be done with a home-made claw grip improvised out of a six-inch nail and a four-inch length of broom handle. Heat the nail and hammer it through the wood; while the nail is still warm, bend over the top two inches.

Fences that can be climbed are often protected at the top by a secondary wire barrier whose effects are to impede, entangle or injure. These types of wire include razor wire, barbed wire and rolling drums. Razor and barbed wire can be overcome by using the 'batman cloak' method. This 'cloak' can be made out of any thick matting, carpet or heavy canvas. Before climbing you fasten it like a cape, around your neck, where it cannot get in the way of your ascent. When you reach the top it is an easy matter to throw it over your head and release it at the neck, so that it covers the wire. You are now protected from the wire as you go over.

Electric Fences

It is unusual for POWs to be enclosed by an electric fence, but it is always a good precaution to check. To do this, take a small blade of grass and, holding it in your hand, place the tip against the fence. Make sure that no part of your body touches the fence. If you feel nothing, push the blade of grass forward until your hand is within a half inch of the fence. If you do not feel a tingling sensation by this stage, you can be assured that the fence is not live.

Note: some modern electric fences have intermittent pulse

cycles. In these, the pulse cycle may be short and there may be breaks between the pulses.

Tunnels

Tunnelling as a means of escape proved popular in the POW camps of World War II. However, these tunnels took a long time to construct and relied on having enough men not only for the digging, but also for the distribution of the dislodged earth from the tunnel.

Tunnels are still a possible option for the POW today, but they are best kept to less ambitious projects, such as a short tunnel under a fence that can be dug quickly and easily.

INVENTIVE METHODS OF ESCAPE

People desperate to escape from some situation will often do so in a dramatic way, risking not only their own lives but the lives of their families as well. Whilst researching this book I have come across forty such attempts from all over the world. Some attempts were simple enough, but others were downright dangerous.

The one that stands out in my mind was the family from East Germany who were attempting to escape the clutches of communism and flee to the West. Their first attempt, using a home-made air balloon and a platform, failed. On their second attempt they found themselves floating silently on their precarious platform across the minefield and border fences to their goal.

Once escape has been effected, the next priority is evasion. This can either be short-term or long-term. In a short-term situation, the evasion will last only hours, or at the most, days. It can come about either by a soldier's separation from his unit or his having been captured and escaped while still in the battle area. In these cases, the soldier does not have to be so concerned over food and water, and he should still be fit and have a good sense of direction. His main priorities should be stealth and alertness. Long-term evasion lasting weeks or even months can often be the case facing a downed pilot or escaped POW. The main priority in this situation will be survival: food, water, shelter, staying healthy, and being able to travel great distances, often through hostile terrain, in order to return to safety.

If a POW escapes and is recaptured, he can expect to be punished in some way for his 'disobedience'. It is therefore a good idea to stay free. In escaping the camp, the POW can either lie up in a hidden spot until the initial search is over, or he can get out of the area as quickly as possible. At this point, the POW must remember that not only the military, but also civilians may be on alert for any sign of him. It is best that he avoids any human contact with the local population and stays hidden as much as possible. In this case, night-time becomes an ally – most of his travel being done in the hours of darkness. A disguise could also be employed.

BASIC RULES

The following will help to facilitate a successful evasion:

1. Preparation Before Escape.
   Get ready for the escape both mentally and physically. Make a practical plan, deciding on direction and route. Think of all the things that could go wrong and be prepared for any contingency. Have patience and confidence.
2. Escape and Survival Equipment.
   Try and keep back items of food, turning them, where

practicable, into survival rations. Never throw anything away – it could come in useful later.

3. Remember and Observe the Basic Military Rules of Covert Movement.
   Make full use of camouflage and concealment. If possible, choose a route with good cover, otherwise move only when you are sure it is safe to do so, or at night. (See travel section.)

4. Always be alert and don't take chances.

DOGS

Dogs can be a great threat to the escaping POW in two ways. First of all, watchdogs, and even normal domestic dogs can give away your presence. Secondly, professional dog handlers and their dogs can detect and pursue you, possibly leading to your capture.

Dogs have been used for military purposes throughout history. They have been used as guards and trackers by the Egyptians, the Huns and the Romans, amongst others. And for as long as dogs have been used to track escapees, escapees have used evasion methods. These have probably changed very little throughout the centuries.

The Dog

Irrespective of breed, any dog used for military purposes must conform to certain requirements. Below is a guide.
Physical:

Height in shoulder:	22–26 inches
Weight:	45–100 pounds
Speed:	25–30 m.p.h. over short distances

Temperament:
Intelligent, courageous, faithful, adaptable, energetic.

Breeds:
Alsatian, Dobermann, Rottweiler, Mastiff, Labrador

Sensory Characteristics

A dog's vision, although good, is not its primary sense, unlike humans. It is, however, drawn by movement, and if that movement seems interesting, the dog will investigate with its more acute senses of hearing and smell. Some have suggested that dogs have better night sight than man, but there is no evidence for this claim. It may be, that as the dog is lower to the ground, what it is looking at is better defined in its outline.

Dogs hear twice as well as humans and can often hear noises that their owners can't, especially within the high frequency end of the spectrum. Their range of hearing will decrease in bad weather such as heavy wind and rain.

The dog's primary sense is that of smell. Estimates calculate it to be seven to nine hundred times greater than that of a human. As we see with our eyes, dogs 'see' with their noses, putting together scent pictures from even the most microscopic traces of substances or vapours.

The Scent Picture

The scent picture is mainly composed of two elements: ground scent and air scent. Air scent is composed mainly of the smell that an individual human gives off. This is made up of not just body scent, but also the smell of the clothing, deodorant, other toiletries and even the chemicals in the washing powder used to wash the clothes. It also depends on the human's constitution, activity and mental state at the time. The air scent given off by a running POW will hang in the air for a little while before it disperses.

The body scent is also part of the ground scent picture. The dog can pick up another signature on the ground as well. Whenever a person walks or runs he creates an impression upon his environment each time his foot hits the ground. This is caused by the vapours released when vegetation is crushed, dead insects disturbed, and the surface of the ground becomes broken. On average, ground scent can be tracked for up to forty-eight hours, although this time may be extended under favourable conditions. Favourable conditions for a good scent picture are light rain, mist or fog, damp ground, humidity, vegetation and forests. It is more difficult for a dog to detect a scent picture in areas of sand and stone, wherever it is arid, on streets and roads and during heavy rain or high winds.

The Guard Dog

The purpose of a guard dog is to defend a location and his handler. He does this by being able to discover any intruder, find them and seize them. The guard dog may be either running loose in a compound, on a running wire, or on a lead controlled by the handler.

The Tracker Dog

The tracker dog uses a scent picture to detect and pursue a man on foot. Unlike the guard dogs, who work mainly with air scent, the tracker dog works mostly with ground scent – usually the freshest. The dog and the handler work as a team, and for success to be achieved, both must have faith in the other.

Dog Evasion

It is very hard to escape from pursuit if the dog has seen you. However, if you 'freeze', the dog may lose interest as you are no longer moving. If this does not work, there is little you can do but defend yourself. If the dog has not seen you and you manage to get away, you may be able to employ several methods that can be used to delay the dog and its handler.

1. Run at a steady pace.
2. Climb up, or jump down vertical features.
3. Swim rivers.
4. If you are in a group, split up.
5. Run down wind.
6. Do things to confuse the handler.

One way to confuse the handler, is to cross an obstacle, such as a river or a ditch, walk along it for a while and then cross back over again for no apparent reason. If this action is repeatedly carried out, although the dog will faithfully follow your trail, the erratic action will confuse the handler making him think the animal has lost your scent and the search will be called off.

Attacked by a Dog

If you have a strong stick to hand, use it to bar the dog's initial attack, as the dog's instinct will be to paw down the barrier. As well as a defence, it will slow him down if he is running at you. An attacking dog will try to bite you and achieve a 'lock' on you, so if you can manage to pad an arm and offer that to the dog, all the better. Once the dog has seized you, you can use your free arm to try and stop it. Whatever method you use, whether stabbing it in the chest, or hitting it over the head with a rock, it has to be a permanent result, otherwise the injured animal will become even more aggressive. You could also try to break the dog's confidence by doing the unexpected and charging at it shouting, screaming and with your arms stretched. Your greater size and aggression may challenge the dog's sense of security just enough that he will back off, suddenly unsure of his quarry.

It is not wise to use pepper or any other chemical means to distract the dog as this will only add to the scent picture. If you are fit you could try to outrun your pursuers, as the dog will only be as fast as the handler. If you do find yourself cornered by the dog and the handler give yourself up unless you are armed. If there is no other chance of escape, avoid killing the dog as it will probably earn you some unpleasant treatment when you are recaptured.

> **SAS Tip:** a charging dog, with its combined weight and speed, will knock you to the ground. You will stand more of a chance if you can slow him up. A good method is to stand next to a tree or some other object, and then wait until the dog is just feet from you. At the last moment, dive behind the object, causing the dog to slow up in order to turn. This gives you a few extra moments that can be taken advantage of.

SURVIVAL

The shock of your situation and the possibility of capture will cause a flow of adrenalin that will help you to survive and stay free. Use all the skills you have learned from your training to stay unseen and alive. Find food, water, and use your navigation skills. Keep yourself clean and maintain an inner feeling of pride in yourself. Try to live like a native of that land. If you use the environment to your advantage your chances of returning to friendly territory will be high.

In this survival section, you will find useful information, which, coupled with your basic skills, some brainpower and the instinct for improvisation, will prove invaluable in a tight situation.

BUILDING A SURVIVAL KIT

Upon passing selection, you will need to build up a good survival kit. Along with your knowledge of survival skills and techniques, it will stand you in good stead when faced with unexpected situations. Your personal survival kit is very important and should be carried at all times as part of your belt kit. Although you will be issued with some escape and survival equipment, you still need to construct your own kit, choosing the contents with regard to the type and location of operation.

Obviously, you will be limited in how much you can carry and compromises may have to be made. All items must initially be considered before making a choice, weighing usefulness and adaptability against bulk and weight. Every item must earn its place, increasing your chances of survival or escape. Bear in mind that the kit may be your only initial resource and should also be the key to opening the stores of natural resources. It will also catalyse your mind into thinking about how to use the items with the skills you have learned.

Below is a list of some of the possible items that a survival kit could contain, and also a brief note on their use.

A PERSONAL SURVIVAL KIT

Special Matches

These special matches, packed in an airtight container are either waterproof, windproof, or both. When ignited they burn for up to twelve seconds and will not go out, even underwater. Now commercially available, they can be obtained from any good camping or outdoor pursuit shop. They can also be found in ration packs.

Flint and Steel Firelighter

This standard piece of equipment, apart from being durable and dependable, will light thousands of fires in all types of weather.

Tampon

The cotton in a tampon provides the best tinder for lighting a fire. They are now standard issue in the survival kits of RAF pilots. Tinder supply is as important as the spark when making a fire. The cotton wool will accept the spark better if it is blackened with old charcoal first.

Candle

Candles are not windproof, but a four inch one will give you light for up to three hours and weighs less than one ounce. For dual purpose, choose a candle made from 100 per cent stearine (solidified edible animal fats), so that it may also be used as a food source in an emergency.

Contraceptives

The condom is an extremely valuable survival item with many uses. Its main worth is as a water carrier, having a capacity of 1.5 litres when extended to a length of 30cms. To get the best use out of it in this way, it has to be filled correctly: water must be poured in, it cannot simply be dipped into water. To support its water-filled weight, the condom should be held in a sock or a shirtsleeve.

Needle

A needle is of use not just as a sewing implement, but can also be magnetized and improvised as a compass pointer. The best type of needle to carry is one with a large eye and about two inches long (e.g. Chenille No 16, or a sailmaker's needle), as this will be robust enough for the sewing of heavy materials such as shoe leather, rawhide or canvas.

Compass

A good quality compass is a vital kit item. Due to its small size, a button compass makes the ideal choice.

Survival Bag

Windproof, waterproof and capable of preserving body heat, this piece of survival kit could prove essential on operations where hypothermia and frostbite are potential risks. Further protection from conductive heat loss can be achieved by laying the bag on insulating materials such as bracken, straw or grass. Not only are they good at stopping loss of body heat, they also can be used in shelter building or water collecting. The green or camouflaged polythene bags are probably the best choice for your personal survival kit.

Wire Saw

A good quality wire saw in your kit will allow you to cut through wood, iron, bone, plastic and almost any other material. This makes it an extremely valuable item to have. For it to be of any real use, it must have at least eight strands of wire.

Water Purification Tablets

These tablets will kill any bacteria present in water and are quick and easy to use in comparison to other methods. Unfortunately, they do not remove any dirt and the resultant treated water will taste quite strongly of chlorine. The optimum number to carry in your kit is fifty. Each tablet will purify about a litre of water in ten minutes.

Knife

The 'Rambo' type knife might be great for carrying on your belt, but you will require something a little smaller for your survival tin. During selection, a pocket knife is such a useful tool that it should be carried as a matter of course. The Swiss Army knife, with its extra blades, scissors, screwdriver and other implements is an ideal choice.

Snares

Three metres of brass wire make approximately four snares, but you will be better off to include ready-made snares as well. These are cheap enough to buy and work better.

Razor Blades

Razor blades have a wide range of cutting uses, from skinning game and gutting fish to making weapons. They are standard issue for most military survival kits. As long as you are careful and don't cut things beyond its capability, the blade will last a long time and give good service. It can also be magnetized and used in an improvised compass.

Parachute Cord

Like a farmer who never leaves the house without some string in his pocket, so the survivor should always carry a length of Parachute cord. It is extremely strong, with a breaking strain of about 250 kilos. The outer layer is braided over a stranded inner layer of thinner cord. This can be pulled out and used for fishing or as thread. The optimum amount to carry is about fifteen metres.

Flares

Flares are the best way of signalling attention. A launch pistol and up to nine different coloured flares are housed in a standard flare kit. When firing flares, make sure to point upwards before launching.

Survival Fishing Tackle

A basic fishing kit can consist of about thirty metres of line, five hooks (size 14 or 16) and swivels, and ten weights (iron or brass). A float can be improvised using a brewer's cork. This cork, if charred, can double up to provide face and hand camouflage – useful when hunting. If you can fit it in, a plastic luminous lure may also be added.

Survival Medical Kit

Some form of medical kit should always be included, but the items chosen should take into account your skills in this area. Include at least one large wound dressing. I was never without one throughout the whole of my military career and there were several times when I had desperate need of it. Even after use the cotton wool inside can be re-used as a valuable source of tinder.

ASSEMBLING AND PACKING THE KIT

The aim is to keep your survival kit as small as possible, which can seem almost an impossibility with the wide range of equipment available. You must make sure that each item's function is not duplicated by any other item.

Once you have selected everything you require pack them in a waterproof container. There are many things that are suitable for this purpose.

- A metal tobacco-type tin.
- A waterproof plastic box.
- A re-sealable polythene bag in a heavy-duty plastic pouch.
- A snap-seal plastic container (of the type used to pack tablets).
- A screw-top metal cylindrical container.

Whatever is used, once the kit has been packed, the container should then be sealed up with adhesive polythene tape.

SAS Tip: this kit should not be opened again until it is required. Of course, this rule does not apply when you need to modify the contents due to the type of operation or journey that you are being sent on.

DIFFERENT OPERATIONAL AREAS

In the desert your survival kit should reflect the priorities of water collection and navigation. Some means of signalling should be included. In a cold environment, such as the Arctic, include items that will provide warmth, shelter, and if there's space, extra fishing kit. Insect repellent makes a good kit addition in the jungle.

Remember, if you are embarking on any activity or operation that may result in a survival situation, always take your survival kit with you. *Keep it on your person at all times.* If capture is imminent, try to conceal individual items about your body and clothing.

CHAPTER SIX

Fighting in Different Terrain: Jungle/Desert and Arctic

Soldiers in the SAS are trained to fight in almost any terrain. The type of terrain will dictate what you carry and how you operate. For example, there aren't too many rivers to cross in the desert, and it would be extremely unwise to try and take a vehicle through the jungle. This chapter aims to give you an insight into the differences you can expect, to squash a few myths, and again add a few special dos and don'ts that the Regiment will expect of you. As jungle training is part of selection, this chapter deals for the most part with that environment.

JUNGLE

The SAS often operate in tropical regions and so jungle training will automatically be given. The jungle is a hostile environment, full of dangers not only from the enemy, but also from the thousands of different insects, animals and plants. To be able to survive, patrol and remain hidden in the jungle, requires special skills. Even a small team will find movement in the jungle to be slow and laborious. You will learn a range of skills developed by the Regiment that stretch back over forty years. If entered into in the right frame of mind, this training can be both enlightening and pleasant.

There are different types of jungle to consider. The Far East, Malaysia and Brunei has jungle that, provided you work with the environment and not against it, is fairly good. In fact, not only should you be able to cope with your surroundings, you may even begin to enjoy them. The jungles of South America, and Belize in particular, are another matter. Everything seems hostile, including the trees.

Both jungles have their dangers and inconveniences. 'Wait a while' plants are spiky vines that continually grab at your clothing. If you struggle and thrash around you will become more enmeshed. Simply keep calm and remove the offending vine. Snakes are generally not too much of a problem, as they tend to stay out of your way. If you step too close to one that hasn't detected your presence, it may bite. If this happens, try to kill the snake and retain it for identification so that its toxicity can be determined. Ants, spiders and other bugs are also often worried about, but if you are minding your own business, then they will usually mind theirs too. Even so, it is still a good idea to sit on your bergen when you rest. One of the more uncomfortable threats to your survival in the jungle or in tropical lowlands will be the leech. In these conditions they are plentiful, so check you legs and feet frequently. If you have included a heliograph signalling mirror in your survival kit, and find yourself alone, use it to check your back for leeches. If any have taken hold, just knock them off – don't worry about the old stories that they will leave their heads behind and become infected. If they have a good hold apply a lit cigarette or a little salt and they will fall off. Check your footwear before you put it on. Boots and shoes make ideal homes for many nasties, and they can get quite resentful if they find your foot intruding into their nice new domicile.

The jungle is a great equalizer of men, or so they say. However, the way individuals perceive the jungle may be different. Some will see the wall-to-wall foliage as a claustrophobic nightmare, whereas others will regard it as an adventure play-ground. It smells. It is noisy with the calls of birds and animals. Everything is growing or dying, and even in death, you will see life as it grows out of or feeds on the decay. Pick up a handful of dirt from the jungle floor and you will find that it contains a myriad of different insects, all struggling for survival. The whole place seems to move with life.

The other thing that you will notice about the jungle is that it is wet. Even when it is not raining, the high degree of humidity will make you sweat, so that your clothes will be permanently drenched and you will begin to stink. Wash, but don't use soap. Even if you can't detect the slight perfumed smell of a soap bar, an enemy attuned to the jungle will.

Despite the above descriptions, jungle life can at times be quite comfortable, depending upon your tactical situation and your objective. If you find yourself staying in one place for a few days, a routine can be established and some improvements made in your standard of living. If your tactical situation allows for chopping wood, make yourself a pole bed. If not, you can put up your hammock instead. If it is raining or rain is immi-nent, put up your basha first. That way you'll keep your sleeping place and bed dry.

The resources of the jungle are extremely bountiful, and you should never have any lack of building materials. Most of what you need should be close at hand, so it is important to select your campsite carefully. Use the following as a checklist.

- The presence of nearby food and water.
- Stable ground away from swamp, or infected areas.
- Protection from danger, such as rotting or falling trees, wild animals and the like.

The best type of shelter will have a raised platform, as most of the troubling insects and reptiles live close to the ground.

Even if your time or resources do not allow for an entire shelter to be built off the ground, then ensure that at least your bed is. I once tried sleeping on the ground in the jungle – never again!

Bamboo is plentiful in the jungle and is an excellent building material capable of forming the basis of shelters, pole beds, cooking and drinking utensils – even a raft. However, care must be taken when gathering it. Bamboo shoots grow very tightly together and some sections will be under strain which means that sometimes, when you cut it, a section will suddenly spring forward and hit you with considerable force. As it can also be very sharp, this presents a considerable hazard. Vines are also plentiful in the jungle and useful for construction. To collect these, pull them down from the branches, making sure to look up for any hazards above your head.

IMPROVISED POLE BED

My advice is to build the bed first, then construct your shelter over it. A pole bed is a real necessity and can be constructed from bamboo or small branches. These can then be covered with palm leaves or other foliage. If any size material is available, then use that for the base.

HAMMOCK

A good hammock can be made out of a parachute. However, do not try to make one out of vines as they normally break. I recently tried out a new all-in-one jungle-sleeping unit. It consists of a basha sheet, (jungle type poncho) from which a hammock is suspended, and a fitted mosquito net which prevents the little critters feeding off you during the night. It is quick to put up, and, if time and conditions allow, the base of the hammock can be converted into a pole bed. All in all, the new system is a great improvement on the old one, both in terms of style and weight.

JUNGLE SHELTERS

If you intend to stay in one place for a while and have the time to do it, it is worth while making a jungle shelter. Use your imagination and the resources around you and you will soon make a very comfortable dwelling.

FIRES

Cooking is normally restricted during operations. If you do it, use standard issue Hexy-fire blocks. If it is possible try and cook undercover, especially in the rain. Make sure that your shelter doesn't catch fire. If you are located in a permanent site, then it is usually permissible to build a fire for cooking, heating water and other things. At night a fire can also be used to keep away biting insects.

> **SAS Tip:** if you find a termites' nest to set fire to, it will produce great quantities of smoke which will drive away the mosquitoes... if it doesn't drive you away first. Spreading old ash around your bedding and campsite area will reduce the number of insects visiting you during the night.

Once you have got your basha constructed, you have a dry place where you can cook and eat. One SAS tip, as well as a long tradition, is to supplement the standard army rations with strong tasting seasoning or spices, such as curry powder. Before you eat complete any military tasks that need doing, such as communications, weapon cleaning, etc. Leave putting on dry clothing or your 'Zuit' suit until it is nearly dark and there is no chance of your moving elsewhere. If you keep one set of clothes dry, then you will always have something dry to sleep in. Bear in mind that you are going to have to put your cold wet clothes back on in the morning. If it is raining, or likely to during the night, tie pieces of string to the straps of your hammock. These will divert the water from running down the straps of your hammock and forming a pool under your backside.

The jungle may be a hostile environment, but if the soldier works with and not against it, life will be a little easier. Finally, even if you are cold, wet and miserable, you can have the satisfaction of knowing that nothing moves in the jungle at night. At least you will get a good eight hours' sleep.

JUNGLE TRAVEL

It is nearly impossible to travel through the jungle in a straight line. You will have to make use of streams or rivers, game trails, dry watercourses or ridge crests. Cutting through thick foliage is both time consuming and tiring. Make use of native trails if you come across them. If you do this, you must remain fully on the alert as the enemy may also be using them. When you travel in dense jungle, you can expect to make slow progress – five kilometres a day would be making very good progress, although some days you may find that you have only managed to travel 300 metres. On days like these it becomes very tempting to find a path going your way. Don't do it. Most paths in the jungle lead either to or from places where people live, and they are very likely to be used by the enemy in times of war. At night-time jungle paths and trails are used by animals, so do not use them outside of daytime hours.

A different set of SOPs apply to the jungle and you will be expected to remember and use them without fail. On the first day of any insertion, a good patrol commander will run through contact drills with his team and these will be practised silently and frequently. During your travel through the jungle you will come across obstacles in your path: these can be divided into two types, human and natural. Natural obstacles tend to take the form of rivers, gorges and mountains. Human obstacles tend to be anything from hostile villages to enemy troops or positions. Obstacles such as these can slow you down or even force you to change route.

RIVERS

Rivers are generally the most common obstacle you will encounter in the jungle. Whether wide and slow or narrow and fast flowing, both can cause difficulties. In some cases, especially during the planning stage of your insertion, it is a good idea to examine where rivers are situated and determine whether it would be a viable option to use one as a source of transportation. In an emergency, you may be able to construct a raft of bamboo or another light wood and use this as a quicker means of transport.

Using vines and other materials readily available in the jungle, it should be reasonably easy to construct a simple raft. To steer the craft, use punting poles at the rear. Any supplies and equipment should be tied down securely so they are not lost if the boat capsizes. Do not overburden yourself: if you fall into the water, you might find that you are unable to swim.

RIVER CROSSING TECHNIQUES

Any wet area, such as a riverbank or swamp, is surrounded by thick vegetation, which may force a detour. If you are forced to ford the river to continue, choose your crossing point with care. Try to find the widest, slowest part of the river, avoid bends as the water flows too fast around them. Wade through and do not attempt jumping from stone to stone if there are 'stepping stones'. These tend to be slippery and often unsteady, and the slightest slip could give rise to a disabling injury, such as a sprained ankle, or loss of vital equipment.

One of the most common ways to cross a river in the jungle is to secure a line between the two banks. This is taken to the opposite bank by the first man, who should also be the strongest swimmer. When making his way across, he should also carry a stick with which he can probe the riverbed along the crossing route. Once the line is up, each man should use his karabiner to clip on to the line before crossing. Once the first man is across, cover can be provided from either bank.

My favourite river crossing technique is to waterproof the bergens and then clip them all together to form a sort of flotation aid. All the patrol can then swim across together in safety, which is particularly good if the team has an injured man or a poor swimmer. The only downside to this technique is that the patrol is vulnerable at this point to enemy fire. The Regiment has experimented with many different ways of crossing a river, but this does not mean to say that they are all good or tactical. Some have also been decidedly dangerous – so take care.

HUMAN TRACKING TECHNIQUES

The jungle is a bit like a maze. Often, the dense foliage prevents people from seeing each other or even being aware of each other's presence. The only way of knowing whether or not someone else, i.e. the enemy, is out there is to develop visual tracking skills. This skill was first evolved by man to help him find animals to eat. But tracking skills are also useful in the tracking down of an enemy. The SAS have developed this talent to a great degree, and the member of the team with the greatest knowledge of visual tracking usually takes the role of lead scout.

The use of visual tracking in recent military history proved especially useful in the Vietnam War, where it was used by various covert special forces to follow and obtain intelligence on the Vietcong. A visual tracker may also use external help. Dogs were very popular in the 70s and 80s, but electronic devices and helicopters have to a large extent taken over. Nonetheless, the basic skills can still be very useful.

SIGN

'Sign' means the tell-tale marks left behind after humans have passed through an area. There are many types of sign that a tracker may look for.

Temporary Sign

Unavoidable marks left on the ground that are temporary because, after a short time, weather and vegetation growth will alter and cover the area. Examples of temporary sign are: disturbances of the earth, leaf and stick covering, dead insects and the disturbance of wildlife.

Permanent Sign

This type of sign lasts longer. The cutting or breaking of foliage, droppings or man-made objects left behind are a few examples.

Top Sign

Signs fall into two visual ranges, top sign and ground sign. Top sign is generally found in vegetation above knee height and is usually caused by a human walking through the undergrowth. The more men walking through the foliage, the more top sign there will be, and therefore the easier to follow. A broken branch at shoulder height is a typical example.

Ground Sign

This is seen as a disturbance in the substance of the actual track or path that the tracker is following. Young growing plants trodden down, footprints, scuffing of settled fallen leaves, skid marks left by people climbing up or down hill are examples of ground sign. As with the top sign, the larger the group of people being tracked, the greater the ground sign.

Temporary Small Ground Sign

- Bent, broken, disturbed or squashed sticks and leaves.
- Freshly disturbed earth and worm casts.
- Sand on leaves, rocks, etc.
- Shadow or shine on leaves.
- The absence of spider webs (these are normally covered by dew in the morning).

Above left: For those attending selection, fitness is a must, but good map reading is also a vital element in passing selection. Understanding the map and taking the best route all save time and produce higher grades.

Above right: Running with a heavy bergen all day is not easy. Make sure that yours fits well, is comfortable over a long duration, and that it is watertight. The Brecon Beacons are notorious for their bad weather. The secret is to push the pace without actually burning yourself out. Trust the map and compass.

Below: The Story Arms in the Brecon Beacons, a well-known location by all those who have attended selection.

Top: The beige beret of the SAS. All those who successfully pass selection will receive their beige beret with its famous winged dagger – as any SAS man will tell you, it is a special moment and a fabulous feeling! The blue stable belt is normally worn with daily barrack dress.

Middle: The famous 'Killing House'; a flat, square, brick-built building that hides its real purpose. Inside, the building is split in two by a central corridor. On either side are a series of rooms, each of which can be configured to represent just about any combat scenario. The left-hand rooms are mainly used for basic shooting skills while those on the right create room-combat situations.

Bottom: The AR-15 was designed for the Armalite Company in the late 1950s. Later the US Army called it the M16A1 and it became the standard rifle in the Vietnam War. However, even before Vietnam, it had been used in combat by the SAS in Borneo. The M16, constructed of pressed steel and plastic, was among the first of the modern-style rifles, firing the smaller 5.56mm ammunition as opposed to the standard NATO 7.62mm round. The M16 is still the preferred combat rifle of the SAS, especially when combined with the 203 grenade launcher.

Above left: You would be surprised at the amount of different weapons used by the SAS. Many have been designed for silent killing, as with the crossbow shown here. Designed and built by Ivan Williams of Shropshire, this all-metal weapon is lethal up to 100 metres.

Above right: Range work is not restricted to the 'Killing House'; the SAS use many different ranges both at home and abroad. There are ranges where dummies will talk to you and even ranges where vehicles can be driven. The latter allow for the practice of live firing anti-ambush drills.

Below: Although all new members are required to be parachute trained, Air Troop specializes in freefall and other methods of flight. HAHO (High Altitude, High Opening) is a technique which enables men to be dropped, deploy their canopies and glide some 30 kilometres to their target. This method is particularly good for cross-border insertions. HALO (High Altitude, Low Opening) drops allow the patrol to fall in close formation with their parachutes opening at a pre-set height, normally around two thousand feet. This increases the accuracy of keeping the patrol together at the landing zone.

Room-combat training is not just restricted to the SAS. Those people most at risk
from acts of aggression, such as the Royal Family and senior politicians, attend
Hereford for demonstrations at which they are encouraged to take part. This picture shows
Prince Charles and Princess Diana sitting very close to targets while the
SAS burst into the room firing live ammunition.

The four-man patrol, which survives to this day, was formed during the Borneo campaign.
Each team member will have a skill allowing them to perform and operate under very
hostile and difficult conditions. Such arduous tasks, in enemy territory, produce tough,
self-reliant men, who are capable of living in the jungle or surviving in the desert.

Left: If you are a captured soldier, your very existence may be under threat. How you react to that threat will depend on the training you receive. The SAS take interrogation training very seriously.

Bottom left: Being captured as a prisoner of war must rank as one of the most frightening experiences a soldier can face. The immediate fear of the unknown, the threat of death, or at best a severe beating, will affect your emotions. And the very nature of your predicament will fill the mind with a sense of isolation and abandonment. This can only be overcome with realistic training.

Below: The personal survival pack is of the utmost importance to every SAS soldier. They will carry it whenever the possibility of a forthcoming survival situation exists. The choice of contents is crucial and will vary according to the type and location of operation terrain. You will be well advised to make your own survival kit before attending selection; even seasoned SAS soldiers have perished on the Brecon Beacons. Your decision on the items to be included in the survival kit can only be made after careful consideration. You must assess every item's usefulness, its adaptability and its weight or bulk.

A full heli-borne assault by SAS troops on a bus. The anti-terrorist team cover just about every scenario and option. The main aim of such training is to evaluate both equipment and techniques. If something is found to work, the next step is to become skilled at the procedure in order to reduce the amount of time it takes to reach the terrorists. Timing, speed and accuracy must be balanced in order to save lives and complete the task.

It is difficult to travel in a direct line through jungle terrain. Although there are game trails, ridge-crests and native paths, you should where possible avoid them. Likewise, cutting your way through the vegetation is exhausting and slow and could alert the enemy. The SAS soldier must worm his way through dense jungle, a process that can be very slow.

Top left: River-crossing in the jungle can be very dangerous, albeit mostly unavoidable. If you must cross, choose the widest, slowest point, where the water is shallow. Avoid bends, as the speed of the current will increase when wading from the inside of the bend to the outside. So will the depth of water. Wade through rather than jump from stone to stone.

Top right: The lead scout has the responsibility of alerting his patrol to any possible enemy activity, as well as having to navigate the patrol to its objective. Due to the fact that lead scouts are often the first point of contact with enemy forces, they are usually armed with a weapon capable of substantial firepower, such as a light machine gun, a semi-automatic shotgun or a rifle fitted with a grenade launcher.

Above: Skiing is a military skill required by the SAS squadron assigned to the Northern Flank during a major conflict. It is also a great way of learning to ski properly. Race teams, as seen here, are encouraged to increase speed and proficiency.

There is nothing better than to spend several weeks climbing in the mountains, whether it is in Wales or Southern Europe. Those new to the regiment, with no previous experience, will be taught the basics of rock climbing and abseiling techniques, before attending courses in Europe. Two SAS members have succeeded in climbing Everest.

Canoeing may seem like fun, but in rough seas it can also prove very dangerous, as several members of the SAS have found to their cost. Boat Troop activities include learning just about every method of entry by water. If that means being launched from the tube of a submarine, then so be it. This picture show two SAS soldiers in a 'Klepper' canoe during an exercise off the Welsh coast.

Permanent Ground Sign

- Man-made items, sweet papers, string, clothing.
- Cut branch, stick or vine.
- Large skid marks.
- Camp fires.
- Human secretions.

FACTORS WHICH INFLUENCE TRACKING

- Spoor: depending on the size of the party being hunted.
- Terrain: it is easier to track through jungle than mountainous areas.
- Sun and Rain: slowly destroys and erodes the spoor.
- Time: nature will restore the damage.

The spoor can give clues to the identity of the person or persons being tracked, and sooner or later, the tracker will come across a 'tag', such as the tread of a certain print, or the same cigarette butt-ends that will identify a certain individual. If he is lucky enough to find more than one footprint, he may even be able to determine how fast his quarry is going – the faster the quarry, the longer the stride.

SPOOR PROVIDES INFORMATION

- The number of people hunted.
- The direction of the quarry.
- Speed: this will also indicate whether the quarry is injured.
- Type of footwear (Identification tag).
- The intention of the quarry. This will take several days to establish a pattern.

TERRAIN

Each type of terrain has its own advantages and disadvantages to both tracker and quarry. Trails in long grass, especially when it is over half a metre, are fairly easy to follow as the grass will be knocked down. Short springy grass will quickly go back to its original position. When grass is walked over, the pressure will push the leaves one way, indicating direction. The path will present a different colour contrast when trodden. Even if a grass path is well-used, it will still be possible to calculate the time it was last walked over by checking the dew which the night temperatures leave on the trail. Mud previously stuck on to the soles of boots will fall or brush off and will mark the grass.

It is difficult to track over rocky or desert terrain because the ground is so hard and dry. Look for disturbed rocks. Depending on the weather, distinct spoor can be left in sandy desert areas for days. When a rock is kicked, the underside will present a darker colour. On sandstone, boot marks will show up as darker in colour, whereas on lava the marks will be whitish.

Equipment will be easier to see in a rocky or desert environment, and in sandy areas will leave a sign that will be visible for many miles. Footprints can be left in sand. In hard sand these will be clear to see. In soft sand the footprint will go deep and only produce a shadow.

The rainforest is an environment where quarry may leave many signs for the tracker to follow. The undergrowth is very thick and there are many streams and rivers. Signs left behind in wet areas may only be temporary, but they will be sharp.

- Footprints on the soft banks or mud on the rocks.
- Mud stirred up in riverbed discolouring the water.

SAS Tip: before crossing a large river, most soldiers will stop to prepare themselves and their equipment. This will leave heavy sign that the tracker will be able to spot.

TRACKING OPERATION

SAS patrols are often called upon to trail the enemy and then gather intelligence on his activities. To do this, the lead scout must first pick up a spoor to start from. Once this has been done, the tracker can then determine his quarry's general direction. At this stage, he doesn't need a constant supply of sign, all he needs to do is follow the natural lay of terrain. For example, if we enter a house, we normally take the easiest way, such as the door. The same principle applies to walking through thick undergrowth: we normally take the easiest way through. Occasionally, the quarry will leave another obvious sign; for example, when he climbs over a rotting log or leaves a footprint in some soft ground. This is a 'confirmed sign', confirming his direction of travel to the tracker. If the tracker locates an overnight campsite or a rest area, he can gain even more vital information on the enemy.

Campsites can provide a great deal of information. Weapon butts rested on the ground and marks where shelters have been erected can all help to indicate the size of the quarry's numbers. Campfires and food scraps may indicate his physical strength. Vital clues can also be gained by studying rubbish holes and makeshift latrines.

LOST SPOOR

If there is no further spoor and the trail has gone cold, the tracker will know immediately and will then examine his options. If he is still confident that he is heading in the right direction, he may do a 'cast'. First of all he will do a visual cast, checking to see if the quarry has had a choice of opening on the natural line direction. If this produces no further sign then he will backtrack to the last known sign and carry out a 'sweep'. This will generally consist of walking in a circle some metres from the last known sign.

DECEPTION

If the quarry knows he is being tracked, he may well try some tricks to throw the tracker off or delay him. For this to succeed, the quarry must ensure that the time spent in laying the decoys is less than the time the tracker will take in discovering them.

A person walking backwards will present a different sign to one walking forwards. For a start his pace is shortened, and there will be a greater pressure from the toes and ball of the foot than the heel. Loose dirt, sand or leaves will also always be dragged by the direction of the move. If you are employing this manoeuvre, ensure that you walk on your heel and lift your knees high.

Brushing the track will only indicate to the tracker that you intend to change your direction. It is far better to side-step over a distance as this will reduce the spoor to nothing.

Crawling on hands and knees will eliminate any top sign, but is best done along a large animal track. To the tracker, the sudden absence of any top sign may also mean that the quarry is injured.

BOOBY TRAPS

If mines and other military equipment are not available, a booby trap may be an option used by the quarry to slow up the tracker. Again though, the trap must not take any more time to construct than it does to slow the pursuer down. In Vietnam, the Vietcong used a wide range of booby traps, some causing serious leg injuries to the American soldiers which then got infected. The closer you get to the enemy camp, the more the likelihood of booby traps, where they can also be used as an early warning device. These may be quite dangerous, as well as being well concealed. Some may even have bluff trip wires, designed to make the tracker uneasy and more cautious. **Warning**. Information and illustrations of traps shown in this book are done so purely in the context of escaping or collecting animal food.

SPEED

Depending on his fitness, the quarry may try to use speed to gain as much distance between himself and the tracker as he can. This may cause the spoor to go cold and is especially effective on open ground where the ground sign is light anyway. In this case, the tracker must alter his tactics accordingly.

If time is on the side of the quarry, he may also use irrational actions to confuse the tracker. These may include lighting a campfire out in the open, doubling back parallel to the line of your march for a distance or climbing a rock face when it is not necessary. These actions may not only confuse and delay the tracker, it might also make him doubt his abilities. As trackers rarely work alone, this will cause a lack of trust in the tracker's skills and weaken the patrol's morale. Leaving a clear, false trail can also confuse the tracker, as long as it is not overdone. Travelling along a linear feature such as a river before setting off again is also a good strategy. The weather may also be on the quarry's side as direct sunlight, strong wind and heavy rain and the passing of time can all lessen spoor and cause a trail to go cold.

Tracking is a skill learned over a long period of time, but one that is very important in improving the effectiveness of a patrol. Knowledge of visual tracking can give you the added edge necessary to locate the enemy.

SUMMARY

The jungle phase of selection takes place twice a year at the Jungle Training School in Brunei. Experts from several nations, including instructors from SAS Hereford staff this school. The six-week training periods take place in March and September, depending on the selection course you are attending.

'Selamat datang. Silakan,' means welcome, make yourself at home. Brunei is a country tucked in the north-west corner of the Borneo Island, between the Malaysian states of Sarawak and Sabah. It is a tranquil nation, populated by a warm and friendly people. Most of the 277,000 inhabitants are of Malay origin, but the country is also home to Chinese, Indian, and Europeans. Islam is the state religion that co-exists happily with other beliefs, which are openly practised. While Malay is the national language, English is spoken by the majority of people.

Author's Note: if I can offer one piece of advice for those lucky enough to visit Brunei, make sure the directing staff arranges a visit to Jerudong Park. This is an amusement park to equal Disney World, with the exception that there is no queuing and all the rides are free. This more than makes up for the lack of bars and nightclubs.

REMEMBER

- 'Bukit' means hill.
- 'Basha' means your jungle living space.
- 'No cutting' means sling your hammock.
- 'Cutting' means make a pole bed.
- 'Campong' is a village.
- 'Laddang' a cultivated clearing.
- 'Silent routine' means whisper *always*.
- Don't worry about the leeches – just pull them off. Always check after being in the water.
- Snakes will normally avoid you, unless you accidentally sit on one.
- Always tie a bit of string to the support line of your hammock. If it rains in the night your hammock will fill up with water.
- Don't fight the jungle, go with it.

ARCTIC

The SAS involve themselves in Arctic warfare but tend not to say too much about it. There is an annual training trip to Norway, but even with the Regiment this is classed as more of a skiing holiday. But make no mistake, the SAS are trained to a very high level in the skills of Arctic warfare. As well as the Norway trip, other Regiment members are invited on more advanced courses, for example at the German Mountain Warfare School in Mittenwald. This course lasts about a year and is divided into two halves: the first half, over the summer months, consists mainly of mountain climbing skills; the latter half, over the winter months, is mostly skiing (see troop training). Canada is also used for Arctic warfare and winter exercises.

If you get to go to Norway, my advice is to enjoy it. On this trip you will get to learn the basics of skiing and winter warfare, and will also get acquainted with the army issue skis, affectionately known as 'planks'. As their name implies, they do nothing for your beginner's confidence or style. Cross-country skiing is fairly easy to learn and you will spend most of your time skiing through tree-lined routes in central Norway. You will also get some free time when you can get to the local resorts, hire some decent skis and try out the weekend skiing scene. You will find it relaxing and with a good pair of skis you may even find that your skills are really quite good after all.

Once you have mastered the skills of basic skiing, you will also be expected to carry a bergen and pull a pulk (sled, used for ferrying equipment over snow). Usually, by the end of four weeks, you will find that your skiing has become quite proficient, often improved by the competitiveness of the end of the week race. At the end of the trip to Norway, the squadron will normally take part in a major exercise, either with the Norwegian army or as part of a set NATO exercise.

The SAS use a wide array of vehicles in their training in Arctic warfare, and they are very useful for covering large distances and carrying your equipment at the same time. Two popular vehicles are the large 'Bandwagon' and the two-man snowmobile. I would advise you to concentrate and rely upon your new-found skiing skills.

As in all extreme conditions, be aware of the weather and treat it with respect, no matter how excellent the equipment the Regiment has issued you with. Even when it is sunny, temperatures can quickly fall to as little as −40 °C. Human skin begins to freeze at −37 °C, so take care that exposed areas, such as the ears and nose are not freezing. The wind-chill factor is also something to be very aware of, as this will increase the chance of you getting frostbite. Being towed behind a vehicle can increase the wind-chill factor too. For example, if the vehicle is travelling at 20 m.p.h., and the air temperature is −20 °C, the wind-chill factor can cause the temperature on the exposed skin to be as low as −43 °C.

During your Arctic training or exercises with the SAS, you will, at some point, have to live outside for several days, using either tents or snow holes for shelter. Tents are the colder option, so if you have the choice, go for a snow hole. If you do end up in tents, it is advisable to do most of your cooking outside the entrance flap. Many tents have caught fire from a knocked over cooker, including my own. Snow shelters are warmer places but need to be properly constructed. If you have never been in the Arctic, here are some variations.

ARCTIC SHELTERS

Snow shelters come in a variety of forms and sizes, but some take more effort and time to make than others. This is important to consider, especially if you are a lone survivor. The type and depth of snow will also place limits on your choice. The snow trench and the fir-tree snow shelter have already been covered in Chapter Three, but the depth of snow found in the Arctic allows for a wide variety of snow shelters.

The Snow Cave

For this, you will need a snow depth of more than two metres – a drift or cornice is often ideal. You may need some tools in order to dig through the snow, and sometimes the snow may be too hard. However, the important point to remember is to always make sure that the inside of the roof is domed, otherwise you will wake up in the morning with it on your head.

The Snow Igloo

Making a snow igloo takes time and effort to construct, as well as a little skill in how the blocks are placed. It is probably the best option if you plan to be in one location for some time, or if there is more than one of you. You will need cold, compacted snow, and tools – an axe, a knife, and a saw or a spade. It is built from the base up, in a spiral that is angled inwards.

There is a second, and far easier way to construct an igloo, which is an advantage as far as the novice is concerned. First of all, stamp down an area of snow, and then build up a mound of hard, packed snow. When this is the required size, simply tunnel into it. Alternatively, form some fir branches or sticks into a frame and pack snow on top of it. Take care to make your entrance hole on the lee side of the igloo. Even so, cold air will still come in and stay at the base of the igloo, so make sure that your bed is on a raised platform. Placing a lit candle in the centre of the shelter can drastically increase comfort: you will be amazed at the warmth it can provide, even though very little heat is generated.

The Arctic can produce severe conditions, such as 'whiteouts', which means, as in the jungle at night, no one moves. If this happens, stay in your shelter, take advantage of the rest; I can assure you that no one else will be operational in such conditions. A good snowstorm can even be a positive thing when you are in an OP, as it will help conceal it even more. You must be careful, however, not to mess it up by leaving unnecessary footsteps in the fresh snow.

The courses in Norway and at the German Mountain Warfare School have already been mentioned. Promising members of the Regiment may also be offered courses at the Alpine Guides course in Bavaria, or at the French Climbing School in Chamonix (see troop training). These are all worth taking, if you are given the chance.

DESERT AND ROCKY AREAS

The SAS are at home in the desert and have probably done most of their fighting in that environment. However, it would be a mistake to assume that all deserts are the same: some are hot, some are cold, some are sandy and dusty, some are rocky. Major problems arose in the Gulf War just because it was assumed that the desert environment would be hot. In fact, the region had one of the worst winters on record, and the SAS patrols operating behind enemy lines were caught up in a freezing snowstorm. One man died of hypothermia, and others came very close. All this, while the troops in Saudi Arabia were enjoying the sunshine.

Even in a region generally regarded as hot or rocky there may be a variety of climates and flora and fauna. One such area is the Jebel Massif, the high mountainous plateau in southern Oman. The Jebel is an impressive sight, rising high above the coastline and coastal villages. At either end of the plateau, where the Jebel dwindles into the surrounding plains, the vegetation is sparse and the ground barren. In the middle the vegetation is quite lush and beautiful, with grass flowing like ripened grain. The air is always cool and fresh, a pleasant change from the unbearable summer heat of the southern capital, Salalah. It was in this area that the SAS fought for several years.

Deserts present their own particular problems and

scenarios. Contacts usually take place at a longer range and because of this, it is usually the amount of firepower that wins the day. Finding shelter can be a problem, and many factors have to be considered. First of all, be prepared for extreme conditions: deserts may be very hot during the day, but at night the temperature falls dramatically and it can be bitterly cold. Deserts are not only made of sand but may also be made of rock or salt. Nor do they have to be flat – some are mountainous, and some are in valleys. Even the amount of vegetation may vary from none to a surprising variety. Each desert has its own peculiarities and merits. But make no mistake, survival is hard, and building a shelter can be even harder, especially if you are without any material resources.

THE SANGA

This simple shelter is basically a circle made of whatever material is at hand, be it rocks, branches or stones. Once a cover is placed over the top, it reduces exposure to the sun. When I was first in Oman, the Jebel tribesmen used to construct their homes using a method similar to this. Pile the rocks about three feet high, but use extra layers at the bottom to give the construction a bit of strength, then use a poncho, or anything similar to provide a roof (this is best taken down when the sun has disappeared).

GETTING LOST IN THE DESERT

You are unlikely to become lost in the desert while on foot, either as an individual or as part of a group. Technological advances mean that most SAS soldiers now carry a GPS system, which allows them to navigate just about anywhere. However, if you do become lost, then you must face the fact that you are in a serious survival situation. This can happen if your transport fails or if you have just had a contact with the enemy. In most cases, your most sensible option will be to stay put and await rescue.

In favour of this option is the fact that you will be easier to spot if you stay with the wreckage, if that was your last known position. Also, there may be a greater variety of resources for building a shelter, etc. Rescue teams will generally look for you in daylight hours, so if you decided to move away from that spot (using the time of early morning, late evening or night to travel in), you would be sheltering and they may not see you.

Your main priority is to shelter yourself from the sun and the heat. Using any form of cover, for example, a ground sheet, lay it over either a depression in the ground, or any available rocks or plants. If you do not have any form of cover with you, search for any natural cover that will give you some shade or shelter: rocks, rock cairns, caves, ledges. You may also find a dry stream bed, or wadi. Quite often the steep sides of wadis contain caves or crevices, so it is worth looking them over. Keep in mind that whatever shelter you find or build, you must also protect yourself from those other major threats to your survival: thirst and bullets.

The insect life of the desert is not much to worry about; you will probably get bothered by flies, but these are not a real problem and their numbers can be lessened by making your shelter on a site that has a little breeze (a hillside, ridge, or somewhere that gets an onshore wind). There are scorpions about, but they tend to hide from the sun under rocks and will generally not bother you. Even if you do manage to get bitten, the worst you will feel is a little sick.

WATER

A supply of water is vital in the desert, and you must carry and drink as much as possible. In a combat situation your mouth will feel dry most of the time, so if you get the chance, and your supply of water is plentiful, take advantage of it. Experienced soldiers often brew up at what seem like the strangest times – this is because they know that a cup of tea will make you feel wonderful. So, if you see them do it, follow their lead. A bit of salt added to your water will also help. Even under normal circumstances, the body is constantly losing water from its natural functions of breathing, urination, excretion and sweating. In hot conditions, sweating will increase, and so will your body's need for water. Therefore, in any conditions where water may be in short supply, the first priority is to conserve the water already in your body.

1. Cover any exposed skin as soon as possible. This will not only give protection against sunburn but it will also aid water retention.
2. Avoid energetic work during the heat of the day. If you must move, don't rush.
3. Talk only when necessary. Avoid eating much if water is not available.
4. Drink in the cool of the evening, or at night – and then in small sips. Don't swallow hurried mouthfuls.
5. Don't smoke or drink alcohol.

Even these conservative measures are only effective in the short term. It will still be imperative to find a source of water to replace what is being lost by your body. If you do not find one, you will not survive for long, and your only hope will be an imminent rescue. It does not matter if you have everything else – food, shelter, equipment, etc. – without water you are done for. If you find yourself in this situation, it is worth considering making a solar still. This method, beloved of so many survival books is simple, but it does work.

THE SURVIVAL STILL

The solar still can provide a drinkable supply of water if your own supplies are low or if the water you have found is impure. Water can be produced in almost any environment using this method. To make it, you will need a clear plastic sheet about two metres square, together with a water container. A plastic drinking tube, about 1.5 metres long is also desirable.

Make a hole in the ground, about one metre across and about 75cms deep in the centre, where the container is placed. If there are any around, try putting some stalks, leaves and roots in the bottom as well, as they will increase your yield of water. If you have a tube, place one end of it in the container, and then spread the plastic sheeting over the hole, making sure that the other end of the tube is sticking out under its edge. Next, secure the edges of the sheet with rocks and then place one more in the centre of the sheet so that it makes a dip, or an inverted cone. For best results, the centre should dip about 35cms from the horizontal. The final stage of construction is to place soil or sand around the edge to secure the sheet and seal off the hole from the atmosphere.

This method works on the principles of condensation. The sun's heat passes through the sheet and heats up the ground. Any water present evaporates, but the vapour remains trapped by the sheet. This saturates the air with moisture droplets that then begin to condense on the underneath of the plastic. Eventually the droplets will run down along the sheet and fall into the water container. The normal yield, over twenty-four hours, is about half a litre, although you may get less than this in dry desert conditions. In very good conditions you may even get 1.5 litres. If, as suggested above, you used fleshy plant material to line the hole with, your yield will increase to about 2 litres, even in the desert.

There are some points that must be carefully observed during construction.

a. Make sure that the sheet does not touch the sides of the hole at any point, or the water will be lost back into the ground.
b. Make sure that the sheet is clear of the container also, or some water will be sure to run down the outside of it and be lost.
c. Check that the seal around the edge of the hole is complete and airtight.

A single still is unlikely to provide enough water to sustain one man indefinitely.

CHAPTER SEVEN

SAS Squadrons

There are four Sabre (fighting) squadrons within 22 Regiment SAS A, B, D and G. Each squadron consists of four troops, as well as a small headquarters section. The troops are based upon the different methods of insertion, but all are trained to operate in every environment and terrain. The troops are divided into four sections: mobility, mountain, air and boat. Each troop has patrols, which are made up of four men, and this is the basic unit and the backbone of the SAS. Each troop member will also possess an individual skill, such as being a medic or proficient in languages, demolitions or signals, as well as the troop skills. Many members, especially those with long service within the SAS are proficient in several different skills.

INDIVIDUAL SKILLS

The patrol often has to act as a self-contained unit behind enemy lines, so each member has a skill that will complement the others and will enhance the patrol's effectiveness. The medic of the team is highly trained and will often be able to keep an injured person alive until they can be casivaced. In a more peaceable role, they are also important in local 'hearts and minds' campaigns. The signaller has the important task of looking after and operating the communications system between the patrol and base. The linguist is essential in communications with local communities and translations. There will also be a man trained in using demolition skills, for when the patrol is called upon to sabotage any enemy installations.

MEDICS

The skill of the medic becomes invaluable when a soldier becomes ill or injured behind enemy lines. Often, no other assistance is available. SAS medics are trained to a high degree, not only doing an internal course, but also attending one of several hospitals where they are allowed to practise their skills on real patients.

The range of potential injuries is large. From snakebite, to broken bones, to a gunshot wound, the medic must be confident of treating any injury and be able to sustain life until a casivac can be called in. In extreme cases, he may even have to perform surgery or identify and treat a tropical disease. Below, I have included some of the skills an SAS medic will need to know and be able to use under extreme combat conditions.

> **Author's Note:** along with many others, I was shot on operations in Oman. The medic was with me almost immediately, and despite the enemy lashing us with heavy fire, he tended my wounds and lifted me to the helicopter. The pilots came directly into the fight to collect members of the SAS. It was a comforting thought that if shot the skill of the troop medic coupled with the speed of a helicopter casivac could get you to the field surgical team within twenty minutes.

Medics need to be able to first of all assess the situation, decide upon priorities, and then act upon whatever course of action has been decided. Of course, these will all depend upon the situation at the time, but generally, the following rules will apply:

1. Keep calm. However serious an injury or dangerous a situation, panic will only impair the ability to think clearly and act effectively. Time will be wasted – and time can mean life.
2. Do not put yourself in any unnecessary danger. This is not cowardice. Remember that you will be no help to anyone if you suffer needless injury.
3. Think carefully, but as quickly as possible, before you act.
4. Do your best to reassure and comfort any casualty.
5. See if there is anyone else who can help you with the situation – perhaps other uninjured or active survivors. There may be someone there who is also medically qualified or who may have more experience than you.
6. When assessing individual casualties, use your senses to the full to find out about their condition. *Ask, look, listen, smell.* Then *think* and *act.* If the casualty is conscious, ask him to describe his symptoms, to tell you what he thinks happened, and what he feels is wrong with him.

If a casualty is unconscious, first check his breathing by placing your ear close to his nose and mouth. If he is breathing you should be able to hear and feel the breath. If you place yourself so that you are looking down the body, you can also check for chest and abdominal movement. If you detect no signs of breathing, you must take immediate action to ensure that the airways are clear.

Artificial Respiration

a. Supporting the neck with one hand, ease the head backwards with the other. Keeping the head back, tilt the chin upwards. This action automatically opens the air passage and brings the tongue forward so that it does not present an obstruction. Once the head is in this position, check inside the mouth for anything that may cause a blockage, such as dentures, vomit or other materials. Once this passage is opened and cleared, the casualty will often begin to breathe again. If he does, and his heart beat is steady, put him into the coma (or recovery) position.

However, if there is a visible injury to the front or back of the head, or any possible damage to the neck or spine, keep the head tilted back in that position to maintain a clear airway, but be aware of the possibility that the casualty may vomit and therefore block his airway again. If the casualty is to be kept in this position, a collar or head support should be improvised.

b. If there is still no sign of the casualty breathing, he must be given help with respiration. This is best done giving mouth to mouth resuscitation. With the head still tilted back, pinch the casualty's nose, take a deep breath, open your mouth wide and seal your lips over his open mouth. Blow gently into his lungs and watch for the chest to expand. As soon as it reaches its maximum expansion, lift your head away and breathe in and out. You will now see the casualty's chest contract. This procedure ought to be repeated four times, and after this, check that the casualty's heart is beating. Of course there may be some circumstances where mouth to mouth is either not possible or not convenient; in this case, use mouth to nose resuscitation. With this method, the mouth is kept shut and the lips are sealed tightly around the casualty's nose.

It is no use giving oxygen if the heart is unable to pump the re-oxygenated blood to the vital organs. Check for this by feeling for the carotid pulse in the neck. If no heartbeat is detected, then chest compression must be administered, as described below. However, before this is carried out, you must be absolutely sure there is no heartbeat, as chest compression used over an existing beat, however weak, will cause great damage. If the heart is beating, continue giving the assisted breaths at a rate of 16–18 a minute. Once the casualty can breathe for himself, continue giving assistance at the natural rate until he is breathing normally.

Chest Compression

When performing chest compressions, the casualty should be lying on a firm surface. Locate the bottom of the breastbone, or sternum, and measure upwards the width of three fingers. Place the heel of your one hand over that point on the bone, and then lay your other hand over the top of the first. With your elbows straight, lean forward so that your arms are vertical and your weight is bearing down on the casualty's chest. Press down on the breastbone to a depth of about four to five centimetres, before leaning back to release the pressure. Perform fifteen compressions at a rate of about eighty per minute (count one back, two back, three back and so on, leaning forward on each number).

Normally, breathing and circulation happen together. If one stops, the body's organs will not receive the oxygen they need to survive and function. If however, both breathing and heartbeat have stopped, then assisted breathing and chest compressions will have to be performed together. If you are alone, you will have to alternate the procedures. Give fifteen compressions, tilt the head back to restore the open airway and then give two assisted breaths. Then repeat the cycle of fifteen chest compressions to two assisted breaths until a full minute has passed. At this stage, check for signs of heart beat or breathing. If none are present, continue the process as above, checking for breath and heartbeat every three minutes.

If two active survivors are available, they can both assist the casualty: one can give assisted breaths and the other can perform the chest compressions. In this instance, four assisted breaths should be given at the start, followed by five compressions. Thereafter, the pattern should be one assisted breath followed by five compressions. Aim at a rate of one compression per second. Each assisted breath should follow the release of the fifth compression without a pause. As above, a check should be made to see if the heart has restarted beating initially after one minute and thereafter every three minutes. Once a pulse has been detected, chest compressions should be discontinued. When the casualty has regained a heartbeat and the ability to breathe unaided, he should be checked over for other injuries and then placed in the coma position.

The Coma Position

If an unconscious casualty has a reasonable heartbeat, is able to breathe for himself and has no other serious injuries, he should normally be placed in the coma, or recovery position. To put a person in the recovery position, kneel to one side of the victim and turn their head towards you. Straighten the arm nearest to you and tuck it under the victim's body; the other arm should be laid across the chest. Grip the ankle furthest away from you and cross it over the other ankle. Gripping the victim's clothing at shoulder and hip, roll them towards you. Bend the uppermost arm and leg at right angles in order to support the body. Lay the victim's face on its side and check that the airway is clear. Warning: Do not use the recovery position if there is risk of back injury.

The position of the arms and legs will maintain the casualty in that attitude. Sometimes broken bones or other injuries may make it difficult for the limbs to be positioned correctly. In these cases, use padding or rolled up clothing to support the limbs and to ensure that the airways stay open.

Bleeding

Serious loss of blood can be very dangerous and so any bleeding should be stopped as soon as possible. There are three methods that can achieve this aim.

a. Direct Pressure

Take a dressing and place it over the wound, applying firm but gentle pressure. It is preferable to use a sterile dressing, but in an emergency any piece of clean cloth will do. If no dressing is available, use your hand to cover the wound, gently holding together the edges if necessary. However, it is important that whatever dressing you use, it is big enough to cover the wound and overlap on to the surrounding area. If the bleeding is serious, the blood may soon come through the first dressing. If this happens, cover it with a second, and, if necessary, a third. An even pressure can be maintained by tying a firm bandage over the wound and dressing, but this bandage must not be so tight that it restricts the blood flow.

With a large wound, if you have access to a suitable dressing, first bring the edges of the wound together. Use the dressing to keep the wound closed. If the wound is bleeding heavily, use the dressing as a pad and press it into the wound where the bleeding is heaviest. Doing this will slow down or stop the blood loss until the body's natural healing processes start to take over. These defences include:

i.   The fact that blood will clot relatively quickly if the flow is slowed or stopped.

ii. A blood vessel that is cleanly cut will soon shrink, close and retreat into the surrounding tissue.

Sometimes, even without outside assistance, these natural processes will stop the bleeding anyway. Anxiety causes the heart to beat faster and therefore increase the blood flow, so it is important to calm and reassure the patient, and make sure that they rest as much as possible.

b. Elevation

If there are no injuries that can be exacerbated by this action, raise the injured limb as high as possible. This reduces the rate of blood flow to the injured part, and helps the veins to drain the area.

c. Indirect Pressure

When the above procedures fail to stem heavy bleeding, the use of indirect pressure points must be considered. However, this method can only be used to control *arterial* bleeding, so you must be sure what type of external bleeding you are dealing with. Arteries are the blood vessels that carry re-oxygenated and filtered blood from the heart. Arterial bleeding is bright red in colour (rich in oxygen) and spurts out in time with the heartbeat. Venous (from the veins) bleeding is darker red due to its lack of oxygen and impurities. It does not spurt, but rather flows steadily from the wound.

An arterial pressure point is where the artery crosses a bone. There are four main pressure points that are capable of controlling heavy arterial bleeding – on the arms and legs. The ones on the arms are located on the brachial artery which runs down the inside of the upper arms. The pressure points for the legs are found in the centre of the groin along the femoral arteries (which run down the inside of the thighs). These points can be pressed against the pelvis, which is easier to do if the casualty's knee is bent. If you use pressure points, still take the opportunity to dress the wound more effectively.

Pressure Application

i. Locate the fingers or thumb over the pressure point and apply sufficient pressure to flatten the artery and arrest the flow of blood.
ii. Redress the wound.
iii. Maintain the pressure for at least ten minutes to allow time for blood clotting to begin. *Do not exceed fifteen minutes* or the tissues below the pressure point will begin to be damaged by the deprivation of arterial blood.

Although unlikely, you may find yourself in a situation where you yourself may be injured, but conscious and alone. Start to prepare yourself mentally for this event and have a self-help procedure ready:

i. Lie down and rest – out of the wind if possible.
ii. Apply direct pressure to your wound. Put a dressing, improvised or otherwise, on it.
iii. Tie on a bandage tight enough to maintain firm pressure without restricting circulation.
iv. Elevate the injury if possible. Keep as still as possible to relieve pain.

Fractures

The following signs indicate if a bone fracture is present:

- Difficulty in normal movement of any part of the body.
- Increased pain when movement is attempted.

- Swelling or bruising accompanied by tenderness in the area of the injury.
- Deformity or shortening of the injured part.
- Grating of bone heard during examination or attempted movement.
- Signs of shock.
- The survivor having heard or felt a bone break.

Immobilization of the fracture is the only possible course of action when in a survival situation. As with any casualty situation, check there is no immediate danger that may threaten you. Then splint the casualty's fracture before moving him. If a wound is also present with the fracture, remove the clothing in the immediate vicinity and treat the wound first. Of course, the casualty must always be handled gently so that further injury and pain can be avoided.

The importance of a splint is that it supports and immobilizes the area of the fracture so that no further damage can be caused. Using a bit of improvisation, splints can be made out of anything: sticks, branches, a tight roll of clothing or bedding, or even suitable pieces of wreckage or equipment. The splint should be padded and then positioned so that it supports the joints above and below the fracture. If nothing comes to hand that is usable as a splint, then tie the injured leg to the good leg – this will partially immobilize it. When a fractured leg appears to be deformed or twisted at an unnatural angle it may need to be realigned before it is splinted. The casualty must agree to this. Realignment is carried out by pulling gently on the end of the limb to reset or straighten it. Splints should then be applied only when every possible thing has been done to right it.

If possible, the limb then needs to be elevated. This will lessen any swelling or discomfort as well as help to treat the symptoms of shock. Ensure that the casualty gets some rest.

Gunshot Wounds

An interesting fact is that four out of every five gunshot wounds will be in a limb, which will give the casualty a very good chance of surviving. However, any wound from a high velocity missile, be it a bullet or shrapnel, will cause much damage to surrounding tissue. Travelling at over a thousand feet a second, the missile will cause the muscle fibres to be pulled inwards and away from the missile track. This phenomenon is known as cavitation. The process also produces a vacuum that sucks dirt and clothing into the wound, hence maximizing damage and the risk of infection. The amount of damage caused will depend on the energy released by the missile upon impact. Death may occur:

- Instantly – if the missile hits a vital organ.
- Within minutes – by choking or massive haemorrhage.
- Within hours – large wound causing severe haemorrhage and shock.
- Within days – uncontrolled haemorrhage, shock, infection, loss of vital organs.

With a gunshot wound, if you are far from professional assistance, there are two forms of help: self-help, and if you are in a four man SAS team, help from the patrol. Both methods are similar.

First, get the casualty to lie down and keep still. Attempt to stop the bleeding by applying direct pressure to the wound, either using a dressing, or, if none are available, your fist (do not use a tourniquet). If a shell dressing is available, apply it as soon as possible, and if needed, apply several. Give the casualty (or yourself if you are the injured party) morphine.

If the casualty is unconscious, maintain the airway and check that his breathing and heart rate are steady; then put him in the recovery position. Keep checking on his cardiac and respiration rates, but avoid moving him unless you have to. Unless it becomes absolutely necessary, never leave an unconscious patient alone.

SIGNALLER

Maintaining communications is vital to any military operation, particularly within the SAS, who need to be able to pass information back to headquarters. Information can be as diverse as calling in an airstrike or casivac, requesting an extraction or simply passing on routine reports. Without adequate communications, operations would be near impossible.

SAS signallers need to be very skilled in the use of different radio equipment, as well as coding and decoding (Morse code, although taught, is rarely used nowadays). On operations, the signaller normally shares his sleeping space with the patrol commander, so that messages can be quickly sent, received and acted upon. It is also quicker if two people co-operate on radio communications. The set that used to be used within the Regiment was a PRC 319, manufactured by Thorn EMI Electronics, but this may well have been updated by now. This powerful radio, capable of data, voice and CW transmissions, has a 50 watt output and an electronic message system. It has a very wide frequency band, 1.5 to 40 MHz, and is also capable of burst transmission which makes it almost impossible for the enemy to intercept the message traffic.

Another communications system that is commonly used is the compact satellite system known as SATCOM. Although not a new system, the latest models are only slightly larger than the PRC 319 radio. These systems often offer the most secure way of sending messages from any point on the surface of the earth directly back to Hereford. Despite the radio systems getting more sophisticated, they do not seem to reduce in weight, and this is the one drawback of being patrol signaller.

> **Author's Note:** on one occasion, we parachuted on to the Island of Senya, in the far frozen reaches of northern Norway. Here, when it is the middle of winter, the only daylight you see creeps under the canopy of darkness for an hour at midday. We descended into the middle of a blinding snowstorm and it was obvious that the exercise should have been cancelled; it was too late for that, however, and we found ourselves knee deep in snow. For four days that blizzard raged around us and the temperatures fell to below minus thirty degrees, but we struggled on and decided to grin and bear what was considered another 'Head Shed' cock up. We all grew weaker, but for the signaller it became a test of human endurance, due to the weight of his radio set in his bergen. One night, as we struggled our way towards the RV with our rescue helicopter, he collapsed, totally exhausted, in the snow. I struggled to help him up, and eventually we pressed on. He didn't complain once; despite the weight of his bergen and the life threatening conditions, he just gritted his teeth and soldiered on.

Quite apart from the special skills and responsibilities of the patrol signaller, every man in the SAS is trained in the use of a radio. This knowledge can be vital on certain operations, such as in Northern Ireland, or on the anti-terrorist team. Here operations can vary from static ops to foot and vehicle surveillance. In these cases, every soldier will have access to a personal radio or a car radio which will be discreetly hidden. One such system is made by Davies Industrial Communications Ltd, who manufacture covert radios for vehicles, surveillance operators and anti-terrorist teams.

COVERT AND DISCREET VEHICLES SYSTEM

Radios can be concealed in a car so that under normal circumstances they will not be detected. The radio is connected to conductors which can be hidden either in the seat headrests, or in the roof of the car, just above the driver. The operator wears a small earpiece that enables him to hear any messages clearly, and transmissions are controlled by a small presser button. This can be either located near the hands or the feet.

MICRO EAR

This new device is one of the smallest radio communicators ever and was developed out of a combination of unconventional RF engineering and hearing-aid technology. No other receiving device is needed to receive messages other than the micro ear itself. It is self-powered by an internal battery which has a life of about fifteen hours. While allowing a full range of audio functions, it is crystal controlled to a specific frequency. The squelch is automatically blocked if there is no incoming signal, so the receiver will remain silent when not operational. The volume can be controlled, and any background noise is also filtered out, allowing the operator to receive clear messages.

DEMOLITIONS

The SAS basic demolitions course lasts about eight weeks during which the theory is backed up with practical demonstrations. The course offers a huge quantity of information that is often extremely interesting. Much of the course is spent in the classroom, but none of the work is boring. The practical side takes you from the basic rules of handling explosives to actually making them. There are also outings to oil refineries, telephone exchanges, railway stations, etc.

Demolitions skills are especially needed in times of war. Saboteurs will attempt to destroy anything of value to front-line troops, whether it be materials, equipment, food or communications. Destroying installations hits the enemy hard and will help to defeat him. The SAS aim to achieve this objective with as little effort as possible. Learning the complex formulas which will cut steel, as well as knowing the most damaging sites to place them, will be taught on the course. Every potential target has a different challenge in store for the demolitions team: most will be heavily guarded for a start. Having knowledge of the wide number of targets available is one thing, knowing how to plan the attack and place the charges correctly is another.

The first priority of the course is to teach safety. Once this is instilled, you will then be taught about standard British explosive equipment. This is followed by booby trap theory and strategy, as well as explosive ambushes and improvised charges. On this four-week basic course you will also learn to plan a good target recce and produce a report that can be acted upon.

TARGET RECCE

Prior to carrying out a target recce, it is suggested that you gather as much information about the site as you can. Maps, aerial photographs, local information, and any information from prisoners of war will all be useful.

When making your plan, you must consider four things – your route to the target, your route from the target, the time limitations on carrying out the task and the amount of equipment required to do the job. First of all, you will need a sketch map. This must cover an area of 500 metres square and include name of the person who carried out the recce, grid reference, type of target and the date. It should also show all terrain details such as woods, rivers, etc. Enemy defences, obstacles and vehicle movement should be marked, as should suggested routes to the target and LUPs (Laying Up Position). Don't forget to indicate North.

You will also need to make target details. Draw side elevations, cross-sections and dimensions of the target. Also, indicate the sort of material that will need to be cut, e.g. wood, steel, masonry, etc.

You must list the type and quantity of explosives needed, as well as any specialist equipment.

Security details are also important, and you should have a good idea of the enemy's strength, disposition and alertness as well as guard change over times, regular transport visits and the weapons positioned on site.

HANDLING EXPLOSIVES

Strangely enough, modern high explosives are fairly safe to handle unless a detonator has been added. Plastic explosive feels a little like plasticine and can be moulded in the same way. PE4 is white, and, unlike the explosives that preceded it, does not really have any distinctive odour. Detonators come in two varieties: electrical and non-electrical. The basic detonator is an aluminium tube, about 250mm long which is half-filled with a substance known as PETN. An electric detonator will have two wires leading from it and will only be activated when the wires are connected to a battery and the detonator is pushed into the plastic explosive. A non-electric detonator on the other hand, is open ready to receive a length of safety fuse and will be activated when the fuse is lit. Once triggered, the detonator will have a speed of 19,000 feet per second which will cause the PE4 explosive to explode at a rate of about 24,000 feet per second. This force is enough to cut through steel.

SAS Tip: it is not a good idea to carry around ready-made charges with detonators sticking in them as they have a tendency to go off. Instead, the detonator can be replaced with detonating cord. This is much safer; just tie three knots in a length of det cord and place it into the middle of your charge. With this method, you can link a series of charges, and you will be able to handle and fit charges using just one initiation device at the end.

Author's Note: I did my eight-week demolition course in the early days, and found it to be very good. Of course, I learned all the technical details, such as the right amount of explosive to cut steel or concrete. Above all, I learned the basic SAS formula for estimating the amount when all else is lost – 'add P for plenty'. One day, we were loaned a derelict house to practise on by the RAF. The object was to determine the correct amount of explosive with which to blow a hole in the wall. Several of us strapped a frame charge to the side of the house and then I rigged the detonator to the 'Shrike' (an SAS developed device for setting off explosives). To make it even more interesting, we decided to carry out an assault on the house after the hole had been blown. We retreated to a safe distance in one of the adjoining empty houses and I set off the charge. I shouted 'Go Go Go' and we charged through the clouds of dust and debris only to find no hole – in fact no house. It looked like we had over-estimated a little on the amount of explosives needed and now the house had disappeared.

INDUSTRIAL SABOTAGE

Industrial systems need to produce continually if they are to be effective. If certain vital circumstances that allow this are removed then the system can no longer function. When planning an attack on one of these systems the SAS have to take into account what will produce the best long-term results. An industrial system will be kept out of operation for longer if parts of energy are difficult to replace. By this I include the following:

- Raw Material
- Electricity
- Water
- Oil
- Gas
- Transport.

The sites that tend to be targets for sabotage include military airfields, shipping, bridges, roads and power stations. Prime movers such as turbines are normally fairly standard, so it is better to attack the driven machinery. Cast metal is another good target as it will break and be damaged easier than other metals. It must be borne in mind that even if several machines are damaged, it may still be possible for the enemy to 'cannibalize' or salvage the undamaged parts in order to make a new machine. In order to prevent this, the machines should all be hit in the same way, and in the same place. Another good way to sabotage machinery is to either drain the oil or introduce some sand while the machine is still running; it will then self-destruct.

LASER TARGET MARKING

The invention of the Laser Target Designator (LTD) has made it even easier to eradicate a target. Instead of bombing it, or sending in a demolitions team, the SAS only have to see a target to destroy it. In practice, the team on the ground aim a laser at the target and 'paint' it with tiny beads of light. A missile can then be launched, usually from a fighter aircraft, which will be guided by the laser to the exact spot.

THE RAID ON PEBBLE ISLAND

The sabotage raid on the Argentine airfield at Pebble Island did not use laser markers as they were still unproven. Conventional methods still provided spectacular results. On the night of 14 May 1982, forty-five men from the Boat and Mountain Troops of 'D' Squadron were infiltrated by helicopter to attack the airfield. Using standard SAS charges, they destroyed six Pucara aircraft, four Turbo-Mentor aircraft and one Shorts Skyvan. Several Argentine pilots and ground crew were also killed, and the airfield rendered inoperable. Upon waiting for extraction, the team were spotted by an enemy aircraft. This was soon taken out by an American stinger missile, however, and all troops returned safely.

LINGUIST

Many operations will take place in far-off lands where the natives do not or will not speak English. A linguist is of the utmost importance to a patrol. To be able to communicate in the native tongue will often win the support of the local people and assist in any 'hearts and minds' campaign. A linguist is also valuable when interrogating prisoners of war.

While at Hereford, most soldiers are encouraged to attend a language course at the Army School of Languages in Beaconsfield. The policy may now have changed but it used to be the case that a language course was usually followed up by a trip to the respective country. This helped to consolidate what had been learned.

Arabic

Arabic is not only quite easy to learn, it is also very useful, as the SAS have fought many of their battles and done many exercises in Arabic-speaking countries. You will be able to communicate quite well with as little as 500 words since Arabic tends to reuse simple words to communicate a concept rather than inventing a new one. For example, we might say 'holster', in Arabic it would come out as 'house of the gun'. This could be very important when carrying out weapons training with a friendly Arab nation.

Malay

It is no longer as necessary to speak Malay as it was in the past. Britain no longer retains much interest in that region and there is less unrest than there was. Over the past few months I have spent time both in Malaysia and Brunei. It had been some twenty-five years since I last visited, and I was quite amazed at the progress both countries had made. They now have living standards and an infrastructure equal to any society in the West. Most people there can also speak faultless English, although learning Malay will only endear you to these warm-hearted people.

Norwegian

The Regiment maintains a strong commitment to NATO's Northern flank and therefore many SAS soldiers learn to speak Norwegian. A fairly easy language to learn, you will find that with 1000 well-chosen words and a little grammar (the laws of which are not unlike German), you can easily be understood. The important thing to remember with Norwegian is that the tone rises and falls rather like singing. Interestingly, many slang words used in the North of England are similar to Norwegian words – an inheritance from the 'Norsemen' who invaded our shores.

When you enter the Regiment, you may well be offered a language course. I would advise you to take it, not only to enhance your skills, but also to make time spent in that country more enjoyable and fulfilling. You will gain a much better understanding of other countries, and it is also a skill that can still be useful when you leave the Regiment. The linguist, working together with the patrol medic can do much to enhance the 'hearts and minds' policy with indigenous peoples.

They are the front contact in any psychological campaign in converting local tribesmen to accept a peaceful way of life.

TROOP SKILLS

MOUNTAIN TROOP

Mountain Troop specializes in all aspects of skiing and mountaineering. New members without any previous experience will be taught the basics of rock-climbing and abseiling and many SAS soldiers are chosen to attend courses in Europe. The German Alpine Guide course is one of these; it generally takes up two SAS personnel at a time and lasts for a year. For those that pass through it, the reward is that they become excellent skiers and mountaineers. In fact the SAS have become so good at climbing and skiing that they now run their own Alpine training course.

Most members of Mountain Troop will also be required to teach skiing to others within the Squadron during the annual winter exercises in Norway. Again, members can apply to go on advanced ski instructor's courses in either France or Germany. The high standard of and dedication to training often produces world-class mountaineers or skiers, although it is rare to find SAS soldiers in any competitions. Several members of the SAS have even climbed Everest.

BOAT TROOP

Boat Troop, as their name suggests, is responsible for all the skills associated with water insertion. These may include boat work, diving, swimming and even using a surfboard. Cross training with the SBS (Special Boat Squadron) often takes place as many members of the SBS are stationed at Hereford. The SAS also carry out joint operations with the SBS, using the extremely professional SBS for the actual water insertion.

AIR TROOP

The Free Fall Troop within the Squadrons have the reputation of being prima donnas. Unlike the other troops, they maintain a high degree of individuality as they act as the pathfinders for the Squadron. Parachuting skills are taught to all new members of the Regiment. The course involves making four low altitude (200ft) static-line jumps, seven normal (800ft) jumps and two water jumps. Once the basics have been mastered, all SAS members will also learn HAHO (High Altitude High Opening) techniques as this method of insertion means that men can be dropped some thirty kilometres from their target. Air Troop not only train with parachutes but also specialize in other insertion methods such as micro-lights and power-kites. Power-kites are a lot of fun. If you get the chance, I strongly recommend you try one.

HAHO and HALO

On HAHO or HALO drops, the teams will fall in close formation, their parachutes opening at a pre-set height with the aid of altimeter devices. With the HAHO (High Altitude High Opening) technique, the parachute opens almost immediately after leaving the aircraft. When parachutes are opened at this height, the team can travel in their descent for over thirty miles. To obtain a degree of accuracy, free-fall drift, release point and weather conditions must all be taken into account, as must body weight and air temperature.

In a HALO (High Altitude Low Opening) drop, the

parachutes do not open until approximately 2500 feet above the ground. This requires the parachutist to free-fall for most of the way, a method of infiltration that is fast, silent, accurate and tends to land the team in the same spot. The speed of descent in free-fall is fast, but may vary slightly with each individual and the position he holds. For example, in a normal 'delta' position, he will descend at a rate of 120 m.p.h., but in a 'tracking' position this may well increase to 175 m.p.h.

Depending on the tactical situation, the aircraft carrying the free-fall troops can fly as high as 35,000 feet but at these altitudes, oxygen is a necessity. During the flight this is obtained from a central console, but during the drop, each jumper has his own mask and bottle. A bergen, or some other form of equipment, will, in most cases, also be carried and this will be positioned on the back of the thighs, upside down. Once the canopy opens, it will be released, and although it is attached to the jumper by a five-foot line, the parachutist will normally choose to hold on to it with his feet until he is about fifty feet off the ground. If the bergen is released incorrectly, serious injuries will ensue. In case of main chute failure, all parachutists in the British Army carry a reserve parachute.

Free-fall troops normally use the box-shaped RAM Air Canopies which allow for greater manoeuvrability and control over the rate of descent. It is designed to inflate like a wing, the open front and the holes in the internal sections allowing the air to flow into the canopy. Two lines are fastened to the rear corners of the chute, and these are used both for steering and controlling descent. Upon landing, the canopy will come to a complete halt if the lines are pulled down fully. The RAM Air Parachute has a glide ratio of 4:1, which is excellent, although civilian parachutes have accomplished a much flatter rate.

Another method of insertion tried by the Air Troop was to attach a small motor-powered trike to a RAM Air Canopy.

It had a range of up to 180 miles and was easy to fly, despite take-off and landings being scary.

MOBILITY TROOP

Mobility Troop specialize in insertion by vehicles. The SAS's most famous vehicle has been the Pink Panther, or Pinkie. The Regiment decided to paint their vehicles pink for desert warfare after an old aircraft shot down in World War II was found in the desert. It remained undiscovered because the sand had burnished it to a pink that blended in with the surroundings.

The main and current vehicle in use with the SAS is the 110 Land Rover, fitted with a variety of weaponry in case of engagements: GPMGs, .50cal, Mark 19 40mm Grenade Launcher and .30 cal ASPs. Additional armaments include 80mm mortars and Milans. All Land Rovers are fitted for long range use. Mobility Troop will also use other vehicles, such as KTM 350 and Honda 250 motorbikes. The latter is preferred for its quietness.

The Light Strike Vehicle

The Light Strike Vehicle (LSV) is a progression from the dune buggy and looks a little like something from a Mad Max film. Despite this, the Regiment was impressed by its high speed, cross-country agility and the fact that it was cheap to manufacture. It consists of a tubular frame and a powerful engine and accommodates a three man crew and a wide range of devastating weaponry. The chassis was plated against mine damage and for some models, roll down kevlar curtains were even an option. Unfortunately, it didn't live up to its promise during the Gulf War and any prospect of future use was scrapped.

They had a tendency to break down, whereas the Land Rover 110s were far more reliable.

Members of Mobility Troop will spend time on courses doing basic mechanics with the REME and also training in various terrains, from the UAE (United Arab Emirates) to the deserts of America.

CHAPTER EIGHT

Anti-Terrorist Team

Students who manage to pass selection will eventually find themselves on the anti-terrorist team. As this is unique to the SAS it is worthwhile explaining how it is constructed and detailing some of the specialist equipment used. The team is divided into two main groups: the assault group and the sniper group. These groups, together with a small command and communication group make up a unit. Assault teams focus mainly on assault entries, concentrating on all the methods of getting in, be it an aircraft, train or building. Snipers deal with any long range situation that may present itself. Although the two teams exercise independently, a lot of cross training goes on, thus providing the numbers to suit the situation required. The SAS have a vast variety of equipment and training aids that are in close proximity to Hereford and most are in constant use. Several aircraft types are available to practise aircraft entry and assault. There is also access to a complete two storey building known affectionately as the 'Embassy'.

The original anti-terrorist team, (then called the SP team) grew up overnight. It was raised in response to the Munich Olympic Games massacre at the direct request of the Prime Minister after he and other heads of state had attended the G7 talks. Men were sent directly from Hereford to the Rover factory to take possession of the first four white Range Rovers that rolled off the production line. Rumours that the Prime

Minister himself ordered such direct action in the setting up and procurement of specialist equipment contain much truth. Whatever its history, the team grew rapidly and today it is a full Squadron commitment. The SAS anti-terrorist team has also grown in stature. I travel the world giving lectures and promotions on anti-terrorist work, and all those I visit hold the SAS up as a shining example. If it's done in Hereford, then it must be right, is the feeling one gets from other nations. This is hardly surprising considering the Regiment's commitment to overseas training, and the professionalism it displays.

The Squadron is committed full time to the SAS anti-terrorist role, which is normally broken down into teams A and B. One team will remain in Hereford, normally practising in the Killing House and doing internal courses of study. The other team may take part in terrorist scenarios to duplicate the various types of hostage situation. At some stage during the four-month period most SP team personnel will take part in several exercises, covering trains, buses, aircraft, ships and buildings.

During any major terrorist incident in the UK where the SAS are involved, Hereford is normally given the tip-off to stand-by via the excellent network that exists between the Chief Constables and the SAS. Control of all terrorist incidents in Britain is firmly in the hands of the civilian authority. Even when the SAS are on site, they will only act when the situation demands the use of immediate action to stop the further loss of life, and then only when command has been officially passed from the police to the military. That's when the job gets exciting.

All assault team members wear a black one-piece fire-retarding suit on top of which goes the body armour and the weaponry. This is normally a Heckler and Koch MP5 sub-machine gun that clips flush across the chest. Additionally, a low slung pistol is strapped to the leg for back-up or for use in confined spaces. Most actions now involve wearing the respirator: it not only protects against gas, but it also presents an evil head of obscurity to the terrorists. Boots are non-slip and similar to professional climbing boots.

Sniper's dress will frequently be identical to the assault teams, but excellent camouflage clothing is also used. Again the same weaponry is issued, but additionally, they will each have two sniper rifles, one for daytime use, and one fitted with a night scope. The main sniper weapon used when I was last on the team was a Finnish Tikka M55, but this has since been changed for the British Accuracy International PM sniper rifle.

The one invaluable thing the public does not perceive, is the amount of training that goes into creating a skilful shot, be it in the assault or sniper role. The complex shooting demanded in a hostage situation requires dedication, and the ability to shoot from any position in any environment. In conditions of absolute darkness and uncertain surroundings, and to avoid shooting the wrong person, the SAS soldier must identify, confirm and act rapidly. This can only be achieved by constant and rigorous training in realistic conditions. Abseiling down the side of a building in full gear is not as easy as it sounds. Ropes, harness, weapons and stun grenades, have to be cleared rapidly so that the soldier can close in with the terrorists. Specialist equipment can take years to perfect, and are often only developed for a highly specific purpose.

ASSAULT SYSTEM

Anti-terrorist operations require a wide range of equipment designed to enable the SAS to carry out assaults against buildings, aircraft, ships and trains, covering every possible combination of hostage release. The following equipment is provided to protect the assaulting soldier, while allowing him the advantage over the terrorists.

Assault Suit and Overhood

The assault suit is designed to provide maximum protection against injury from heat and flame when worn with the assault undersuit and underhood. A one-piece garment worn under the assault body armour, the suit is manufactured in Arvex SNX 574 flame-resistant/antistatic/liquid-repellent black 210gsm fabric. A full-length two-way zip fastener protected by a storm flap fastens the suit. Panotex knitted cuffing is fitted at the collar, cuffs and ankles to prevent ingress of flame at those points. Patch pockets are fitted to the chest (for use when body armour is not being worn) and pouch pockets to the thighs. Identification patch holders are fitted to both upper arms. The areas of the forearms, knees and shins are reinforced with quilted Arvex fabric containing Panotex flame-resistant felt which provides additional protection against heat conduction should the wearer come into contact with extremely hot surfaces.

Designed to permit full movement of the body and all limbs, the suit incorporates an integral lifting harness. Fitted with a drag-handle, the harness permits the wearer, when unconscious or incapable of movement, to be dragged out of the line of fire to safety.

The undersuit and underhood are intended for use with the assault suit and overhood. Manufactured from Panotex double-jersey knitted black fabric, they provide an air gap between the wearer's skin and the oversuit. They give protection against heat conduction and thermal radiation, as well as additional protection against flame. The undersuit is a two-piece garment comprising a vest, fitted with a polo-style collar and elasticized cuffs, and trousers with elasticized waist and ankles.

Flame-Resistant Socks

Manufactured in Nomex 450 flame-resistant yarn, these medium thickness knitted mid-calf length socks provide a high level of protection to the feet against direct flame and heat conduction when worn inside a leather boot.

Balaclavas

Manufactured in Panotex double-jersey knitted black fabric, balaclavas are available in standard closed-face configuration, with apertures for the eyes and mouth. Balaclavas provide protection against flame for the face when a respirator is not used. A further version is designed for wear over the CT-12 respirator to protect the face-piece.

Assault Gloves

Assault gloves are designed to provide protection for the wearer's hands while still permitting full dexterity of the fingers. Manufactured in black Kevlar/Cordura flame-resistant and waterproof fabric, each glove is fitted with a soft leather trigger finger and soft reversed-calf leather on the palm for protection against friction burns during abseiling and fast roping. Each glove is also fitted with an adjustable tightened strap on the back of the wrist.

Assault Belt Rig

Manufactured in top quality black bridle leather, the assault belt rig is designed to carry a team member's personal weapons and ammunition. It comprises a heavy duty fully lined belt, a pistol holster and two magazine carriers, a grenade carrier holding two stun grenades, and a three magazine carrier for the MP5.

Assault Helmet and Ballistic Visor

In some circumstances it may be advisable for members of the assaulting team to wear helmets. The best of these is manufactured from polyaramid: it has a V50 (17 grain fragment) of 610m/s and provides a high level of ballistic protection up to and including 9mm Geco steel jacketed ammunition with a velocity of 420m/s fired from a sub-machine gun. It can be worn with the ballistic visor, which affords the same level of ballistic protection as the helmet.

Equipped with a liner and triple-anchor point harness incorporating a quick-release chinstrap, the helmet provides excellent protection against injury from impact. The design of the shell permits comfortable wear of ear defenders/radio headsets and the helmet is fully compatible when using a respirator.

Assault Body Armour

Assault body armour is specifically designed to provide a very high level of ballistic protection. Available in differing grades of ballistic protection, it can be adjusted to operational require-ments, it can incorporate groin protector and pockets in front and rear for the insertion of ceramic plates. A ballistic collar can be fitted if so required.

The outer cover of the armour is manufactured in Arvex SNX 574 flame-resistant fabric. This is based on Nomex Delta C fibre, which is also anti-static and liquid repellent. It provides a very high level of protection against flame and burning liquids. The armour is designed to accommodate the CT400 Radio Communications Harness.

Ceramic Plate

The Level III Plus ceramic plate provides protection against high velocity ballistic threats up to and including 7.62 mm × 51 US M61 ball armour piercing and 7.62 mm × 54 soviet heavy ball (Steel Core) ammunition when worn with body armour. Weighing 2.5 kg and measuring 250 mm × 300 mm, the plate can be worn in the front and rear of the body armour.

Tactical Assault Vest

A tactical assault vest provides additional capacity for carrying equipment. Manufactured in black suede leather, the vest incorporates pockets and pouches for further items of personal equipment such as flashlight, hatchet, crowbar, additional stun grenades etc. The vest is of waistcoat-style configuration, fastened at the front by four 'lift-the-dot' fasteners and can be adjusted for size via elasticized lacing on each side.

Weapon Holdalls

Manufactured in double layer 1200 denier black nylon fabric, the weapon holdalls are available for all existing types of sub-machine guns and assault rifles. Fitted with carrying handles and a detachable shoulder strap, they are padded throughout with closed-cell foam to prevent ingress of water and provide protection against impact. Holdalls are also fitted internally or externally with magazine carriers.

CT-12 Respirator

Developed from the S-10 respirator currently in service with the British armed forces, the CT-12 has been produced to meet the requirements of units tasked with anti-terrorist operations. Fitted with the RC670 CS filter canister it provides protection against CS, CR and other irritant gases and aerosols. The rubber face-piece can be fitted with a high quality speech transmitter and the eyepieces with removable coated polycarbonate tinted lenses which provide protection against flash and fragments.

The second canister mount permits fitting of an adapter into which the CT400 communications harness body-worn microphone can be inserted. Alternatively, it can be used with a second filter canister if so required or with a small compressed air bottle giving a short duration air supply in conditions of oxygen depletion. The face-piece is available in different sizes, and the elasticized harness is fully adjustable for head size. The respirator is supplied with a storage/carrying bag and a spare filter canister if required.

Voice Projection Unit

The voice projection unit is a miniature amplifier unit designed for use with S-10, SF-10 and CT-12 respirators. Powered by a standard 9-volt PP3 type battery, the unit is rapidly and easily attached to the diaphragm on the respirator face-piece. When activated by a switch, the unit projects the wearer's voice over a distance of some thirty metres. This device enables hostages or other personnel in the target area to hear clearly any commands being given during an assault.

CT400 Radio Communications Harness

The CT400 radio communications harness is designed to permit team members to be in full radio communication with the rest of the team. The system can be used with the majority of radio sets currently in service and comprises the following items:

Electronic ear defender/radio headset: This unit protects the wearer's ears against damage to hearing from high levels of noise caused by gunfire and explosions at close proximity in confined spaces. At the same time, even when worn under the overhood and underhood, it will permit the wearer to hear spoken conversation and listen to team radio traffic. The headset is connected by a lead to the central switching unit.

Central switching unit/bodyworn press-to-talk switch: All elements of the CT400 system connect to this unit which is normally worn on the front of the body armour and also contains a press-to-talk switch activating the body-worn microphone.

Bodyworn microphone: This is a noise cancelling device normally worn on the front of the assault body armour in the area of the neck and secured by a spring-loaded clip. In the event that a CT-12 respirator is worn for an assault, the wearer inserts this microphone into the adapter in the spare filter canister mount on the face-piece.

Other items of CT400 equipment, which are also available, include the following:

- Team commander's headset: this is similar to the headset mentioned above but is fitted with a boom microphone.
- TASC sniper's headset: This is a single-earphone headset designed for use by team snipers. Fully waterproof, it incorporates a flexible boom microphone and fully adjustable

headband, and is connected by cable to the wearer's personal radio.

Sniper Command and Control System

The Sniper Command and Control System is designed to permit the unit commander to exercise split-second control over the members of his sniper team. The system operates via a highly secure digital telemetry radio link in the following way:

Up to eight-sniper radio stations can be included in the standard system. Each comprises a UHF PRU-22 radio set powered by an integral rechargeable battery with a nine-hour life. This can be extended through the use of an external battery, which can be plugged into the radio, which gives a further twenty-four hours of operation. Indication of a low battery is given by an amber LED display.

The PRU-22 is fitted with a target indicator button unit, which is attached to the fore-end of the sniper's rifle. In addition, it also features two further red and green LED displays. Once the sniper has acquired his target and it is in the centre of his crosshairs or reticule of his telescopic sight or image intensifier, he presses his target indicator button, transmitting a constant signal to the unit commander and informing him that he has the target in his sights. Should the sniper lose the target, he releases the button and the cessation of the signal informs the commander accordingly.

While the sniper is awaiting the command to fire, the red LED display on his PRU-22 is illuminated in the 'Stand By' mode, indicating to him that the radio link with the commander's set is functioning. When he presses his target indicator button the green LED illuminates, informing him that his set is transmitting properly.

ANTI-TERRORIST TEAM

Commander's Radio Station

This comprises a BRU-22 radio set which features eight pairs of red and green LED displays, each pair representing a member of the sniper team. Each illuminated red LED display shows the commander that the radio link with each respective sniper is working properly. As each sniper acquires his pre-allocated target in his sights and presses his target indicator button, the respective green LED illuminates and stays so while the target remains in the sniper's point of aim. Should a sniper lose his target, he releases his target indicator button and the appropriate green LED on the commander's set ceases to be illuminated.

Once all targets are acquired, the commander can give the order for the snipers to fire at the appropriate moment over the separate team voice radio net.

VIU Touch Screen Visual Display

The VIU display is an optional item designed to interface with the BRU-22 and to present a graphic display of the situation. The unit is fitted with a touch screen, which features two pages of information and can accommodate up to eight and twelve targets respectively. The target symbols are ranged along the top of the screen and can be individually drawn by touch into the 'live' area of the screen. The symbols representing the members of the sniper team are ranged along the bottom of the screen and can be moved on to the 'live' area and allocated targets by touch.

While the snipers are in 'Stand By' mode, their individual symbols appear as grey on screen. On switching to 'On Target' mode, their symbols change to black. Similarly, the target symbols appear as grey on the screen until acquired by their respective snipers when they turn black. When all targets have been acquired by snipers who are 'On Target', a 'Totalizer' symbol on the right-hand side of the screen changes colour, notifying the commander that all targets are covered and enabling him to take a rapid decision to give the order to fire if necessary.

Abseil and Fast-Roping Equipment

Abseil equipment comprises the following: abseil harness, designed to be used as a full-body harness, permitting a team member to be suspended for protracted periods of time (i.e. outside a window), this harness comprises a waist-belt harness, and a chest harness connected by a combi-sling.

Abseil ropes are 11mm diameter non-stretch black polyester rope. This is available in differing pre-cut lengths of 50, 100, 150 and 200 metres. Various descenders are used. The ANKA descender is a horned figure eight abseil descender with the lower ring set at ninety degrees to the upper one, eliminating any tendency to twist during a descent. The STOP descender works on the 'fail safe' principle in that it requires the user to apply pressure on its handle for the rope to move through it; release of the handle causes descent to be halted immediately. This has an anodized black finish.

Karabiners: manufactured in high strength aluminium and fitted with locking screwgates, these karabiners have a breaking strain of 3000 kg; both come in anodized black finish. Rope bags are manufactured in waterproof black polyurethane-coated fabric and designed to facilitate smooth deployment of a rope during a descent. They can be used to accommodate ropes in lengths of 66, 100 and 150 metres.

ANTI-TERRORIST TEAM

Fast Roping Equipment

Fast ropes, in 44mm olive drab eight-strand spun nylon, are used with either a spliced soft-eye at one end or a specialist helicopter suspension fitting. They are supplied in 40ft, 60ft and 90ft lengths.

Grapnel Launcher

The grapnel launcher is a shoulder-fired compressed air-powered launcher designed to launch a grapnel carrying a 9mm climbing rope into a target area at ranges of up to 45 metres at 45° elevation and 55 metres horizontally. Alternatively, a lightweight wire ladder can be attached instead of a rope. During building assault operations, use of the launcher enables assault team personnel to make use of upper level entry points from ground level or from roofs or upper storeys of adjoining buildings. During marine operations, the launcher can be used for covert boarding of vessels, being fired from a smaller craft alongside.

Weighing 9.5 kg, the launcher is of 50mm calibre and is manufactured from high quality black anodized aluminium and steel. It is powered by a rechargeable and replaceable 0.5 litre cylinder of compressed air, located under the barrel, which gives three firings at an operating pressure of 160 bar. A rope storage canister is also located under the barrel, forward of the air cylinder, containing a flaking frame into which the rope has been carefully coiled beforehand. This ensures that the rope is paid out smoothly without tangling when pulled from the canister by the grapnel on firing. The grapnel is a lightweight folding type manufactured in high-strength aluminium and fitted with three spring-loaded folding titanium tines. It is equipped with a flexible stainless-steel cable shaft fitted with a rope/ladder attachment eye and covered by a durable protective sleeve. The head of the grapnel and the end of the shaft are fitted with neoprene O-ring seals which ensures that an airtight seal is maintained in the barrel. This ensures that full pressure is retained for maximum propulsion. Total length of the grapnel is 720mm and the weight is 1.5 kg.

Ascenders and Slings

These items are used in conjunction with the grapnel launcher, STOP descender and abseil harness. When attached to the 9 mm climbing rope, they enable assault team personnel to climb up to the target area entry points. The ascenders have an anodized black finish and are each fitted with a black nylon webbing mountaineering sling. Adjustable for length, the sling has a maximum load capacity of 450 kg and is attached to its ascender by a karabiner.

Lightweight Flexible Wire Ladder

The lightweight flexible wire ladder provides an alternative method of gaining access to an entry point in an upper storey of a building or of boarding a vessel from a smaller craft. Manufactured from 3 mm stainless-steel wire covered in matt black plastic, it is equipped with rungs of lightweight anodized black aluminium spaced 300mm apart and has a width of 150mm. Weighing 1.3 kg and with a length of five metres, the ladder can be attached to the lightweight folding grapnel and deployed by the grapnel launcher. Fitted with swagged steel eyelets at each end, it can be linked to ladders of the same type and length with the use of Maillon Rapides.

Assault Ladders

The SAS use an extensive range of assault ladders of differing widths and heights to cater for the majority of operational requirements. These include single section, multi-sectional and extending types in single width, double width and triple stile designs. All ladders are manufactured from structural grade aluminium alloy with deeply serrated rung sections and heavy-duty rectangular sections. All ladders are fitted as standard with non-slip rubber feet, noise reducing buffers on all exposed faces, and are finished in black polyester powder coating with etch primer.

Single section ladders in single and double widths and triple stile designs up to 4.0 metres in length are used. They are the quietest form of ladder available and are ideally suited for gaining rapid access to public transport vehicles, lower floor windows, or for scaling walls. Wall hooks can be fitted to all ladders, as can sniper platforms.

Multi-sectional ladders are mainly in double width or triple stile configurations, and come in a variety of individual lengths forming up to eight metres in height. They can be transported easily in vans or estate cars and provide team capability for two to four personnel depending on length and conditions. They are fitted as standard with heavy-duty channel connectors complete with nylon slides and locking pins. Sniper platforms are also available for use with these ladders.

Extension ladders (multi-level) offer a choice of widths including triple stile, with single and double sliding sections available. They are general access ladders and are available for both team and lightweight use. Standard fittings include full-length nylon slides, quadruple section restraining brackets, over-extension stops and an auto-swing safety clutch. Specific designs are used for siege and anti-hijack operations.

Intervention Vehicles

The SAS use the Range Rover as an assault intervention vehicle (AIV). This is designed to deploy members of an assault team rapidly into a target area which can be anything from an aircraft to buildings. Fitted with an assault platform and ladder system, it can deliver up to ten fully armed and equipped personnel to access points at heights of up to six metres from ground level. In order to provide maximum stability when carrying ten personnel on the platform and side ladders at high speeds, the vehicle's suspension, shock absorbers and brakes have been uprated. Differing grades of ballistic protection are also available to protect the vehicle. The entire vehicle and assault platform/ladder system is finished externally and internally in black. Each vehicle is equipped with internal roll bars and other safety features as standard. The AIV can include siren/public address system, blue flashing lights and a full range of police and inter-vehicle radios.

The principle idea behind the ladder system is to allow mobility, height, speed and flexibility during any assault. The front platform and side-seats mean that men simply have to jump off to be ready for action. Men on the roof can, if the situation requires, be positioned on the ladder ready to enter second-storey windows, or open an aircraft door. Such a system is invaluable during an immediate action where the terrorists have started murdering hostages as it allows for the assault team to act speedily.

Rapid Entry Equipment

The anti-terrorist team has a wide range of equipment designed to enable rapid entry through doors, windows and the walls of buildings. The range includes silent hydraulic cutters and spreaders as well as an assortment of rams, crowbars and axes.

The hand-held ram, for example, is designed to force open inward-opening doors by being swung against the lock area and imparting a weight load of approximately three tons. It is effective against all but reinforced steel doors and weighs 16 kilograms. The door ripper is a lightweight tool designed to force outward-opening doors with the blade being driven between door and frame in the area of the lock. A ratchet mechanism aid overcomes resistance by allowing the blade to be worked behind the door to provide increased force. The 5 ton hydraulic door ram is designed to force reinforced inward-opening doors. Supplied with three sets of claws to suit all standard widths of door from 760mm to 920mm (30–36 inch). The main ram is positioned over the lock area while the secondary ram forces the jaws into the frame. Operation of a valve activates the main ram to force the door open with a maximum force of 5 tons. An additional 11 ton pneumatic door ram is used against heavy secured doors. The ram is positioned on the door with a support plate over the lock area. Operation of a hand pump forces the hydraulic claws into the frame as secure anchors. An air bag is inserted between the support plate and the door, and is inflated with compressed air from a portable cylinder. It comes supplied with a pump, three interchangeable claws for use on doors of widths between 760mm and 910mm, air bag, air-hose, a compressed air cylinder (uncharged) and shoulder strap.

Also available for rapid entry tasks are the following:

Hatton Ammunition

Designed to remove the hinges of doors without the risk of ricochet, these rounds comprise 12 gauge semi-solid frangible slugs weighing 50 grams. Hinges are smashed from their fixings and damage is caused to surrounding woodwork. These rounds will penetrate vehicle tyres, fire doors clad on both sides with metal plate, cell-type doors, 12mm thick Makralon and armoured glass from a range of 1.5 metres. Hatton ammunition can only be used in Magnum shotguns with 3 inch chambers and unchoked barrels.

R.I.P. Ammunition (Close Range)

R.I.P. 12 gauge close-range ammunition comprises cartridges filled with a mixture of micronized CS, an inert powder to add weight and a further non-toxic powder which, on compression and friction, produces a large amount of carbon dioxide gas on exiting the barrel of the shotgun. The mixture is propelled towards the target at very high speed, forming a cloud of incapacitating airborne irritant. The muzzle of the shotgun can be held against any wooden door up to 65mm in thickness and the powder will blast a hole through it, one round filling a room 9m × 6m in size. These rounds will penetrate vehicle windows from a range of 2–3 metres as well as 12mm Makralon, armoured glass at 1.5 metres, wooden fire doors clad with thin metal plate on both sides and cell-type doors.

Wall and Door Breaching Cannon

Designed to provide a non-explosive method of breaching walls and doors, the system comprises an electrically initiated, pneumatically powered, muzzle-loaded smoothbore 280mm calibre cannon firing water-filled 5 gallon plastic containers. The kinetic energy generated by the impact of the container is sufficient to breach a wall but dissipates immediately after penetration and thus eliminates risk of injury to hostage personnel within the target area. The cannon can be carried by two men and can be transported easily by helicopter or vehicle.

Thermal Arc Cutting

Designed for cutting mild steel, including steel under water. The system comprises a 12 foot flexible thermic lance made from Kerie cable, a single 3 litre oxygen cylinder fitted with pressure gauges, a pressure regulator, battery-powered igniter unit and a 3-way valve which switches the system's working pressure on or off. Consumption of the cable during cutting is approximately 2 feet per minute. The maximum duration of the system is 6 minutes. The entire system is portable, weighing only 10.5 kilograms, and is supplied with a shoulder strap and a belt which enables the operator to wear it while cutting.

Technical Attack Equipment

In addition to the equipment required for any assault, the regiment also have a vast amount of specialist equipment which is used to gather intelligence. These include video surveillance systems, rigid and flexible endoscope units for close-up work and a full range of photographic equipment for stand-off work. Almost every team member, especially the sniper, carries night-vision aids.

Planning Briefing and Command

Thoughout the various stages of any counter-terrorist operation, the collation and presentation of intelligence will play a crucial part in any successful outcome. Planning the attack, and an overall view of where his troops are, enables the commander to visualize events as they actually happen. Additionally, he can also predict what might happen. One of the new development tools available to the SAS is the Atlas OPS (Operational Planning System). This is a highly advanced CAD based software product that allows the operator to feed in a 3D visualization of the target and surrounding area. This image, be it a building, aircraft or ship, can be generated in a matter of hours and updated as new intelligence comes in. The image may show floor-plan layout, positions of windows and door, routes to and from the building, adjacent buildings, video, still photographs and so on.

The advantages of such a system are a tremendous aid in assault team planning. It is now possible to place yourself in an adjoining building, look through a window and assess the view from that point without ever leaving the control room. The system allows the commander a 'fly on the wall' interpretation without compromising people on the ground. Data from one workstation can be relayed from even a small laptop so that assault teams can be updated.

Life Support and Medical Packs

In any terrorist action full medical services will be on standby. In addition, the SAS carry a full complement of life-support systems and medical equipment. The equipment is designed to enable unit medics to deal with severe wounds and injuries, including those caused by blast and bullets, as well as provide emergency life-support in a hostile environment where normal services might be in danger. Resuscitation, ventilation and aspiration equipment; intubation equipment; intravenous administration kits are included in the pack, as are dressings, tracheotomy and crico-thyrotemy kits, burns treatment kits, limb immobilization equipment and anti-shock suits, together with vacuum and folding stretchers for casualty evacuation.

TYPICAL AIRCRAFT ASSAULT

Hijackings were common during my time in the Regiment and great emphasis was placed on aircraft assault. Apart from the speed of approach, the aircraft assault technique remains the same as it was during the time I was at Mogadishu. To recount what we did then will give you an insight to a real counter-terrorist action.

A few minutes after midnight on 18 October 1977, I stood with my back to the fuselage of a Lufthansa 737 jet aircraft. This might not seem so unusual other than that the aircraft occupied the centre of the main runway in a communist country. It had been hijacked five days earlier by the 'Popular Front for the Liberation of Palestine' (PFLP) and they had dragged the disoriented passengers around the Middle East, finally coming to rest in Mogadishu airport, Somalia. Low on fuel, the aircraft had been forced to land the day before in Aden, and here the pilot Jurgan Schumann had been shot dead in front of his passengers. His body was thrown out of the aircraft, sliding down the emergency exit chute to land at the point where I was standing.

So here I was in Mogadishu airport, clasping two stun grenades from which I had removed the pins and was about to lob over the hijacked aircraft. Poised, I watched as members of the German Grenzschutzgruppe-9 (GSG9) special anti-terrorist team swarmed confidently over the aircraft, positioning padded ladders silently against the aircraft fuselage. These ladders enabled them to reach the emergency exits above the aircraft wings and entry doors front and rear. Dressed in dark uniforms and armed with sophisticated weaponry, they crawled like soldier ants with a single purpose into their assigned positions.

Turning in the final seconds, I looked behind me at Ulrich Wegener, the German commander now crouched under the fuselage belly, intently listening to the continuous dialogue from the control tower. Here a German cabinet minister now communicated directly with the terrorists in the cockpit of the hijacked aircraft. The plan we devised was simple. Senior German diplomats in the control tower heralded the news of the German government's capitulation, giving in totally to the terrorist demands. They were informed that the Baader-Meinhof prisoners would be released from German jails and that the $15 million would be paid. As a distraction, the control tower was to keep the terrorist leader talking and at the same time the Somali army was to light a diversionary fire at the end of the runway. The fire, about one click away but in full view of the cockpit, was meant to hold the attention of the terrorists. I am proud to say that this was one part of the plan that was my own. The scene was set: twenty-eight members of the GSG9 and two SAS stood balanced in the shadowy glow of the airfield lights.

Suddenly, with a mighty roar a huge fireball whooshed into the night air casting shadows across the entire airfield. The Somalis had lit a fire all right – they had set fire to a tanker full of petrol. I looked back at Ulrich Wegener with an immense smile on my face, but it was squandered on him; he was preoccupied on the countdown for the assault. The last thing I heard him say was 'Three, two, one, Go!' At this, I stepped away from the aircraft and tossed my first grenade over the starboard emergency exit. Within a split second the second grenade was winging its way over the aircraft hulk to burst in a blast of bright light and the roar of a thunderous explosion. I turned just in time to see the starboard rear door swing open and there in the light of the cabin stood one of the female terrorists. Above me, a GSG9 policeman stood on the top rung of the ladder firing a burst from his MP5 sub-machine gun, slotting her with at least half a dozen rounds from a range of less than two metres. It was the look of stupefaction on her face that astonished me. It was as if she was saying 'What the hell are you doing here?' She fell to the cabin floor dead. At the same time, the GSG9 man dived into the aircraft. Turning my attention back to my position on the starboard wing I could see that the first two GSG9 men had successfully punched in the emergency panel and entered the aircraft. The fire-fight raged inside. I heard the dull thuds of two terrorist grenades exploding. I climbed up the ladder and on to the wing where the emergency hatch had been forced inwards and had dropped on to the laps of two passengers. I watched them sitting there motionless with fear, their eyes shut tight. The GSG9 cries of 'Inlegen, Inlegen' ('get down, get down') could be heard among the spasmodic gunfire. The minutes dragged on. Suddenly, the passengers started to exit the aircraft, some trying blindly to jump and slide down the GSG9 assault ladders, others appeared on the wings. The exodus became more orderly and people were helped down on to hard tarmac where ambulances and coaches swept across the runway to receive the hostages. As more people popped out of the emergency exit I gently assisted them to the ground and reached inside for others. Even though the threat of explosion filled the air, both rescuers and passengers worked calmly, moving away from the aircraft to the ambulances. Then the final passenger was eased down and a senior GSG9 officer stood in the rear starboard doorway and bellowed 'They're all out, they're all out – alive!' and with a roar of satisfaction the hijack of Lufthansa Flight 181 came to an abrupt end.

To achieve success in a hijack, it is important to remember the following:

1. Make a single file approach to the aircraft from its blind spot at the rear. Once underneath the aircraft, adopt our first positions and place ladders quietly, erecting them to

the wings and the rear door

2. Position two men from each of the first two leading assault teams covertly on the wings, one team outside the port emergency exit, the other pair by the starboard exit. The back-up assault pairs should be waiting on the top rungs of the ladders.

3. Position an assault squad at the rear area of the plane by the starboard door, and the front portside door. Both squads use double ladders, allowing the left-hand man to open the door, and the right-hand man to shoot. Back-up personnel outside the aircraft co-ordinate the evacuation of the passengers working with the progress of the assault teams.

4. A continuous dialogue should be maintained between the control tower and the terrorist, with the commander listening in to the conversation. Just prior to the assault, the Somali army, for example, lit a fire some 300 metres to the front of the aircraft to attract the terrorists' attention.

5. With everyone in position, and the command given, Alastair Morrison and myself threw several stun grenades over the cockpit and aircraft wings. This diversion allowed vital seconds during the assault. The leading assault teams stood up, punched the emergency exit panels and dropped the door hatches into the laps of the passengers in the mid-section of the cabin. The main doors front and rear opened simultaneously and entry into the aircraft was made. Control of the centre of the aircraft should be taken, moving down the aisle towards the cockpit.

6. Once evacuated the passengers should be moved away to the rear of the aircraft where medical teams should account for their safety.

As mentioned earlier, the 737 is a fairly simple animal. Once entry had been effected to the centre of the aircraft, the starboard assault team gained a clear line of sight to the toilet doors at the rear of the cabin. The port team, moving forward through the economy area, arrived in the first-class section, which leads into the front catering area. Directly beyond this is the flight deck, the door to which is usually closed. The only obstacles the team encountered were this door and the curtains in the catering and first-class areas. The door itself is of light construction easily removed by a solid push, gaining good coverage of the cockpit area. As it turned out, the only real resistance came from the terrorist leader in the cockpit. This did not hinder or threaten the safe removal of the passengers. The whole assault was over very quickly.

Like all good plans, the Mogadishu assault was kept simple, and for that reason it worked.

CHAPTER NINE

SAS Operations

This chapter explains two typical SAS operations in detail, from start to finish. The first concerns two SAS men who went to help save a country, while the other concentrates on the SAS's role in the Gulf War. Note the difference in preparation, insertion, and their successes. This will help define why the Special Air Service is so *special*.

RESCUE AT GAMBIA

On 1 August 1981, Lieutenant Colonel Michael Rose, then Commanding Officer of the SAS, had been out walking in the Welsh countryside. The attendance of numerous Commonwealth heads of state at the wedding of Prince Charles to Lady Diana Spencer meant that it had been a busy time for the Regiment. They had been drafted in to help out with the protection of numerous VIPs as such a gathering of notables had presented many opportunities for terrorists. Now that it was over, the SAS members involved could return to Hereford and relax a little. Rose therefore arranged to take time off, enjoying the company of his children – something rare for the SAS commander. Even now he wore an electronic beeper on his belt, which interrupted this much-anticipated interlude with an urgent summons. With all haste he made his way to the nearest telephone and made a call to Hereford Headquarters. Diane, a telephonist of long standing in Hereford, switched his call to Major Ian Crooke, who was acting executive officer at the time. From Crooke, Rose learned that the small nation of Gambia, a former British colony, was in the throes of a *coup d'état*. Launched two days earlier, it coincided with the absence of the nation's president, Sir Dawda Jawara, who was representing his country at the royal wedding. Senegal, which had a military agreement with its neighbour, Gambia, had already sent troops to combat the rebels. Additionally, Jawara had asked British Prime Minister Margaret Thatcher for help, and she agreed to dispatch a couple of SAS men to the scene. The Prime Minister warned of the need for secrecy as even this modest response, if it became public, could open her government to charges of renewed imperialism in Africa.

Rose first told Crooke that he was inclined to take the assignment himself – always quick at making decisions, and ever politically minded, such skills would prove very useful in Gambia. Getting Rose back to Hereford would require him being picked up by helicopter, and he needed to make arrangements for his children. Eventually Rose conceded that Crooke should choose an available man, select whatever weapons and equipment he would need, and get to Gambia on the first available plane.

The Gambia covers an area of 11,295 square kilometres in West Africa, and is the continent's smallest independent state. It is a narrow strip of land on both banks of the Gambia River, bordered by the Atlantic Ocean on the west and surrounded on the remaining three sides by Senegal. The capital is Banjul, on St Mary's Island, near the mouth of the Gambia River. A low-lying country, it ranges from sandy beaches along the coast to a swampy river valley in the interior. The economy is overwhelmingly dependent on the export of peanuts, which provides most of the country's earnings. The population is primarily Muslim black African, of whom the Mandingo are the most numerous. English is the official language.

English merchants won trading rights from the Portuguese in 1588, and in the early seventeenth century British companies founded settlements along the Gambia River. In 1816 the British purchased St Mary's Island, where they established Bathurst (now Banjul), and in 1843 the territory became a crown colony. The French, who controlled the neighbouring interior (now Senegal), failed in negotiations to acquire the Gambia River settlements, which, in 1894, became a British protectorate. Gambia achieved self-government in 1963 and independence in 1965, under Dawda Kairaba Jawara. It became a republic in the Commonwealth of Nations in 1970. Independent Gambia is notable in Africa as a bastion of parliamentary democracy and political stability. It has maintained close relations with Senegal, with its larger neighbour being responsible for Gambia's defence.

By 1980, the average annual income was only about £140 per capita, and this was on the decline because the local cash crop, peanuts, had fared poorly in two years of extreme dry weather. On the other hand, tourism was on the increase and could have become an important source of revenue. However, such was the state of poverty in Gambia, that the populace started to complain over escalating prices for the basic needs of food. The problem was not helped by the high rate of unemployment. It soon became obvious from the amount of anti-government slogans painted on walls that the government was in trouble. When slogans turned to actions and the president's private yacht mysteriously caught fire, the government finally realized that a coup was being planned. President Jawara discounted the information and flew to London for the matrimonial festivities.

The revolt was provided by the Gambian Socialist Revolutionary Party, which was headed by a young Marxist named Kukoi Samba Sanyang. His given name was Dominique, but when he became a Communist, he changed it to Kukoi, a word in the native Mandinka language that means 'sweep clean'. Sanyang was also among the African radicals who had sojourned in Libya. The volatile Libyan leader envisioned a confederation of Islamic African states under his guidance. He attracted exiled African political leaders of Marxist persuasion to the Libyan capital and plotted to reshape a number of African governments. Gambia, being 70 per cent Muslim, lay within Colonel Gaddafi's fancied Islamic realm.

At 5.00 a.m. on Thursday, July 30, the coup erupted. Muscle was provided by Usman Bojang. A former deputy commander of Gambia's 300 man Police Field Force – a para-military organization charged with preserving order in the tiny country – Bojang managed to persuade or force the contingent based in the town of Bakau to join the coup. This group, which amounted to about one third of the organization, dis-armed most of the loyal police then quickly took over the nearby transmitter for Radio Gambia and moved into Banjul, the capital. On the way, they opened the country's largest prison and distributed weapons from the police armoury, not only to the inmates but to virtually anyone who happened along. Not long after daybreak, citizens and former prisoners alike began rampaging through the streets and looting shops. Soon, a free-for-all erupted. Within the first few hours of the coup, scores of bodies – policemen, criminals and civilians – littered the streets of Banjul. Arriving at Radio Gambia shortly after rebel policemen seized the station, Sanyang closed the country's borders and its airport at Yundum, some fifteen miles east of Banjul. Then he proclaimed a 'dictatorship of the proletariat' and charged the 'bourgeois' Jawara government with corruption, injustice, and nepotism.

Most Europeans and Americans working in business or

holding government posts stayed off the streets. Other foreigners and tourists stayed in the capital, or kept to their hotels
in the nearby communities and Bakau and Fajara. Many rebel
Gambian policemen, who saw no profit in harming Western
individuals, guided anxious foreigners to the residence of the
United States ambassador, Larry G. Piper. The house was soon
haven to 123 nervous guests, 80 of them American citizens.
A number of European tourists also sought shelter in the
Atlantic Beach Hotel on the outskirts of Banjul, along the
nation's beautiful sea coast. During the trouble, two armed
looters raided the hotel, ransacked the safe, and took the local
manager hostage. As they fled the hotel, gunshots were heard
and the two looters were shot dead in the hotel doorway.
Fearing more looters would arrive and hearing the constant
firing outside, the hotel guests organized watches and posted
guards, 'armed' with fire extinguishers.

President Jawara had made contact by telephone with his
vice president, who had taken refuge in the police headquarters
in Banjul, protected by loyalist troops. In London, Jawara
wisely made himself accessible to the press, and in doing so,
he was able to downplay events at home. Because of this, the
plight of the Europeans and Americans trapped by the situation
never reached the outside world. Had it done so the coup
would have attracted far more attention than it did. For the
first few days of the coup, Jawara controlled all news of Gambia
from London. Acting as if to resume control of the government, Jawara boarded a jet bound for Dakar, capital of Senegal.
In a statement made before leaving, the President talked about
invoking a mutual assistance treaty that Gambia had signed
with Senegal some fifteen years earlier to fend off external
aggression. Yet at this stage no foreign agitator had yet been
identified as having backed the coup.

Around this time, Ian Crooke and an SAS sergeant, Tony,
(not his real name) had chosen and assembled their weapons

and equipment. These consisted of German-made Heckler and Koch sub-machine guns, Browning 9mm automatic pistols, and a stock of ammunition and grenades. Crooke managed to pass his little arsenal through customs and baggage checks and on to the first flight available. This plane happened to be an Air France commercial flight to Dakar. Although firearms can be carried in checked baggage aboard such aircraft, explosives are normally prohibited. But most anti-terrorist teams have direct contact with each other and after several phone calls the normal channels are ignored. This is not uncommon. During the Iranian Embassy siege in London, the German GSG9 commander Ulrich Wegener, had been allowed to view the incident. Upon his return to Germany aboard a scheduled passenger flight, it was discovered that he was in possession of a weapon. Informal contacts within the British diplomatic service cleared the way in minutes. As always, Ian and Tony were dressed in casual attire, attracting no attention from their fellow passengers, among whom were many reporters and television camera crews.

Upon arriving in Senegal, Ian Crooke encountered his first obstacle – British diplomats. Despite the brief from the Prime Minister, Margaret Thatcher, directly to the SAS, the diplomats refused to allow them to get involved. With fighting going on between the rebel forces and Senegalese troops, and with a considerable number of British citizens in danger, officials in both Dakar and Banjul decided that it would only complicate their duties further if the SAS were to get into the act. This would allow them to applaud the Senegalese if the intervention succeeded or to chastise them if it failed. The SAS travel on many missions around the world, normally working close to their counterparts in VIP protection. Accommodation and reception into the various countries is normally handled by British diplomats, who generally shudder at the thought of having SAS men in their company.

With no word from Thatcher, in whose service he had come to Africa, Ian Crooke decided to go ahead with his mission despite the remonstrations of these relatively minor officials. Adopting the policy of out of sight, out of mind, the two men managed to get seats on a plane bound for Gambia's Yundum airport. Upon arrival he met up with the Senegalese paratroop commander, Lieutenant Colonel Abdourah-man N'Gom, who had established his headquarters in the confines of the airport.

Crooke met up with Clive Lee, a hulking six foot six retired SAS major who was employed as a civilian adviser to the Gambian Pioneer Corps, a division of the Field Force that trained rural youth in agricultural and construction skills. Hearing of the coup on the radio, Lee had rounded up twenty-three Pioneer Corps members, armed them, and set off for Banjul (you can't keep a good SAS man down when he smells a fight). To get there from the Pioneer Corps base in the town of Farafenni, sixty miles east of the capital, Lee had to cross the Gambia River. Because of the hostilities the ferry had suspended operations. As with Ian Crooke and the diplomats, this was no time to pussy-foot around and soon the ferry captain had been persuaded to take Lee's band to the other side. Once across the river, they made their way directly to Banjul, moving through mangrove swamps to avoid rebel positions along the main road to the city. In Banjul, Lee's party made for police headquarters, where they reinforced a small contingent of loyalists and set about defending their enclave by barricading the nearby streets.

For the Senegalese troops, capturing Yundum airport had not been easy. During a fierce battle almost half the 120 paratroops making the assault were wounded or killed. Once this task was completed, Senegalese soldiers entered Banjul and within a few hours had cleared the capital of rebels. They had also gained control of Denton bridge across Oyster Creek which prevented insurgents from re-entering the capital from their concentrations in Bakau and Fajara. A combination of these actions secured the route from Banjul to the airport.

The SAS has a very loose connection with its ex-soldiers, most of whom are scattered around the world, mostly working in some security job or for a foreign government. In such circumstances it is expected that should the need arise and their services be required, they are honour-bound to render all assistance to the SAS operation. During the Mogadishu hijack, an ex-SAS officer named David Bullied helped considerably while the aircraft was in, so it was with Clive Lee in Gambia – and there are many other untold instances. The SAS brotherhood bond is extremely strong.

On arrival, they found the situation little changed. Although N'Gom continued to strengthen his forces in Gambia and occasionally traded shots with the rebels, the military situation had reached an impasse. His troops were stalled outside Bakau because Sanyang had taken more than a hundred hostages. The most valuable captives were Lady Chilel N'Jie – one of President Jawara's two wives – and a number of his children. In addition, Sanyang held several members of the Gambian cabinet. And although N'Gom had wrested Radio Gambia from Sanyang's rebels (the transmitter lay between the airport and the bridge), the coup leader had commandeered a mobile transmitter from which Lady Chilel appealed almost hysterically to Senegal, announcing that the hostages would be executed unless the paratroops withdrew. Sanyang repeated the threat himself. 'I shall kill the whole lot,' he warned, 'and thereafter stand to fight the Senegalese.'

On 5 August, Crooke decided to make a reconnaissance. The blue jeans-clad SAS officer and his two associates slipped forward from Senegalese outposts and set out on foot. The weather was hot: during August in Gambia, temperatures routinely exceed 90 °F. Three Britons carrying sub-machine guns could hardly escape notice in Fajara, but the outing was not as dangerous as it might seem. Although there was always the chance that an encounter with an armed insurgent could end in gunfire, the rebels did not seem inclined to harm Europeans. Furthermore, Crooke observed an unmilitary laxity among the troops manning rebel positions. Unknown to both Crooke and the outside world, Bojang had been killed during the second day of the coup. His absence and the resulting lack of leadership probably accounted for the apparent decline in rebel vigilance. Crooke's sortie confirmed that the insurgents were now capable of little more than token resistance against well-trained Senegalese troops.

Crook persuaded N'Gom to begin an advance on Fajara and Bakau the same day. The British officer and his companions accompanied a contingent of Senegalese troops along the hot byways of the suburbs. Peter Felon, a British engineer employed by an American crane company, saw the party when they appeared at his hotel in Fajara. 'Ten Senegalese troops and a British Army officer arrived at the hotel,' the engineer recalled. The officer, probably Clive Lee, wore khakis with no insignia. 'With him were two men who I can only describe as the most vicious looking professionals I have ever seen.' Upon being told that rebels were hiding along a creek near the beach, the pair set off to find them. 'There was sporadic violent gunfire,' said Felon, 'then the two men walked calmly back to our hotel.'

A US aid worker at the American embassy was one of the foreigners who had taken refuge in Ambassador Larry Piper's house. It was early afternoon, he remembered, when a lookout they had posted announced that soldiers were coming up the hill. 'The house,' said the aid worker later, 'was on a bluff sloping to the beach. I went out and saw a wave of Senegalese come running up the hill in full camouflage-type gear led by three whites, one of whom had on an Australian hat, khaki shorts, and a knife strapped to his leg. It was literally like living in a movie.' After ascertaining that everyone was all right and leaving behind a dozen or so paratroops for security, the party disappeared.

Arriving at the British High Commissioner's offices, Crooke learned that armed rebel guards had escorted President Jawara's wife and her four ailing children – one of them an infant of only five weeks – to a British clinic the day before. Doctors at this tropical disease research facility, which stood only a block or two from the High Commissioner's office, treated the children and advised her to bring them back within twenty-four hours.

The interval had passed, and now Lady Chilel had returned for follow-up care. This information came by way of a telephone call to the High Commissioner from the British physician attending the children. The official told the doctor that armed SAS men would be there within minutes, and Crooke and his two companions quickly headed for the hospital.

Hearing that help was on the way, the doctor began to draw out his treatment. The wily physician even convinced the woman's armed escorts that they were frightening his other patients and persuaded them to put their guns out of sight.

As Crooke approached the hospital, he noticed two armed guards posted at the entrance. Handing his sub-machine gun to his companions, the major gave them an order to circle behind the guards. He then walked up to the pair and distracted them in conversation as the other two SAS men crept up from the rear. It is difficult to imagine what Crooke could have said or how devious a plan he might have formulated in order to draw the guards' attention away from his accomplices – the SAS is mute on the topic, following the lead of the British and Gambian governments in their steadfast refusal to acknowledge that Great Britain had sent any military assistance at all – whatever Crooke's ruse, it worked. The two guards froze when they felt gun muzzles at the back of their heads.

Leaving the captives in the hands of his able assistants, Crooke slipped inside the clinic. He surprised Lady Chilel's weaponless escorts as they watched the children being treated and promptly took them prisoner. After conducting the president's wife and children to the High Commissioner's office, Crooke and his party retreated to N'Gom's headquarters at the airport.

A day earlier Senegalese troops, who now numbered about 1500, had found and destroyed the mobile transmitter that Sanyang had been using. Although Sanyang himself escaped, he was no longer a factor. With the silencing of its leaders, the coup's backbone was broken. Many hostages still remained under rebel guns at a police barracks, and disorganized bands of turncoat policemen and criminals had to be rounded up.

N'Gom paced his advance slowly: panic among the rebels might cause them to begin killing their prisoners. They had nearly done so a few days earlier when a policeman who had been forced against his better judgement to join the coup began shooting some of the rebel guards. He was killed in a trice, but his brave act seemed to thwart the planned execution. The Senegalese paratroopers edged up to one side of the barracks, leaving several exits unguarded for the rebels to flee. After a tense hour or so the hostages walked free, and the insurgents dispersed, only to be captured later. Eight days later the rebellion was all over, but it had caused over 1000 deaths. President Jawara was once again the unchallenged and elected head of the Gambian government. Kukoi Sanyang was eventually arrested in the neighbouring country of Guinea-Bissau, but the socialist government there later released him, despite Gambian requests for his extradition. Senegalese troops captured more than a hundred of the rebels and convicts, seven of whom were ultimately condemned to death. Libya was never connected directly with the coup attempt.

In Banjul, the President posed for reporters, hugged his baby son and pronounced: 'I'm relieved and happy.' He answered questions about the rescue of his wife and children by European soldiers with a cold shrug of the shoulders and said that all such claims were much exaggerated. To make Jawara's political recovery as easy as possible, all official comment about the counter-coup and rescue was reserved for African governments. The only confirmation of the SAS presence came from a Senegalese officer who told reporters that SAS personnel had indeed participated in restoring order. As always, the British government remained silent.

The SAS party hung around Gambia just long enough to satisfy themselves that British citizens would be safe and then made their way home. The operation in Gambia demonstrated how a few skilled and confident soldiers can influence an event far out of proportion to their numbers. They could disappear, as if nothing had happened – throwing yet another cloak over the SAS myth. Ian Crooke gave a wonderful detailed account of the whole incident to a full assembly of the Regiment. It was the highlight of an annual debrief, where other members of the SAS found out what everyone else had been doing around the world. As was normal, it was SAS personnel only. Although the British government refused to admit involvement, it was recognized that the success of the action hinged in large measure on Crooke's initiative and good judgement. That he had a lot of help is undisputed. It came partly in the form of the military incompetence of the coup leaders and partly from the presence of the Senegalese. N'Gom's troops supplied the manpower needed to fight rebels who were disinclined to surrender and to maintain security in areas that had been swept clean. Nonetheless, Crooke was the one who tipped the balance. He chose to ignore the restrictions placed on him

by British diplomats and acted as he believed the Prime Minister wished. Had he been wrong, he would have no doubt
suffered severe consequences. But in those days, the SAS were
very much Margaret Thatcher's blue-eyed boys.

GULF WAR

Kuwait sat there like a ripe fruit waiting to be plucked, rich
and complacent with its huge reserves of oil, fantastic wealth
and a port on the Persian Gulf. Virtually defenceless against
external attack, it should have been obvious that the greedy
eyes of Saddam Hussein of Iraq would one day turn towards
it. The Iraqi leader was hungry for Kuwait's money, oil and
land and was determined to take them. After all, there was no
question he could fail with such a ruthless and efficient war
machine at his disposal, and indeed he was proved right: twelve
hours after his soldiers crossed into Kuwait, the country was
his.

Saddam Hussein had not perhaps expected such an international response to his invasion, but that was what he got.
Saudi Arabia, alarmed at the dictator's expansionist ideas,
allowed the American lead coalition forces to base themselves
in its country in order to prepare to retake Kuwait. By 12
November 1990, the build up of coalition forces was going
well: hundreds of thousands of coalition troops were preparing
themselves for battle as the fighter aircraft practised in the skies
above the desert. With so many aeroplanes taking part in the
air campaign, the region was soon to have one of the busiest air-
traffic control systems in the world. Ships from the various
navies patrolled the oceans – some with their Tomahawk missiles already trained upon Iraqi targets. And of course, in
among all these preparations, another group was also getting
ready to go to war: the SAS.

The exploits of the SAS in the Gulf War have been documented in quite a few books during the past few years; most of these have focused on the story of the ill-fated Bravo Two Zero patrol. However, many other SAS operations took place that have not enjoyed such public scrutiny, even though they were successful. One of the first tasks that the SAS was given was to rescue the hundreds of Western and Japanese hostages seized when Saddam Hussein invaded Kuwait. The Iraqi dictator's intention was to use them as human shields and propaganda campaigns. Few in the West can forget how the women and children were displayed on TV, or how the men were taken to strategic sites to deter coalition bombing raids. The very fact that the hostages became spread out in different and often heavily guarded locations made it difficult for any rescues to be attempted.

The SAS were given the task of going deep behind enemy lines and sabotaging vital equipment, especially scud-missile launchers. Mayhem would be caused by their destructive tactics and large numbers of Iraqi troops could be diverted in an attempt to discover the culprits. After hasty preparation training in the United Arab Emirates, the SAS were divided up into mobile fighting columns which consisted of motorbikes, a Unimog and eight Land Rover 110s, all heavily armed. Mobility Troop trained the other members in desert driving skills, and none were harder to master than that of riding a motorbike in the desert. These were mainly used for scouting missions, but took considerable skill and concentration to ride.

The Unimog was the pack animal of the column; carrying rations, fuel, ammunition, water, NBC (Nuclear Biological and Chemical) gear, equipment and spares. Land Rover 110s, all bristling with weaponry, became the teeth of each column. As standard they carried a Browning .5 heavy machine-gun, but their arsenal also included GPMGs, American Mark 19 40mm grenade launchers and Milan anti-tank missiles. The Milan was fitted with thermal imaging sights, which enabled it to be used at night at distances of up to 8 kilometres.

One of the SAS members takes up the story:

'Our column was sent to hunt 400 kilometres or so into Iraq, making our way up the Euphrates into the southern central region. As this was what the SAS was so well suited to, general morale was very high. Provided we followed our SOPs, any contact with the enemy would be on our terms and not theirs. The evening before we deployed we came to the sudden realization that this was all real and that some of us would end up in serious trouble, maybe not even come back. Friends visited friends in other fighting columns, shook hands and made the odd joke: it was a strange mood that evening. Others sat around, checked their weapons and equipment and secreted their "blood money" about their person. This consisted of approximately £1200 in gold coins and a "blood chit" written in Arabic, English and Farsi, that promised £5000 to anyone helping a British soldier. To prevent any opportunists stealing one of these, the soldier had to be alive and the serial number of the "blood chit" had to check out with the soldier's name. All SAS personnel were issued with "blood money".

'Fire-power is an extremely important factor in any real engagement, so the amount of equipment carried is vast. For myself, I carried an M16 assault rifle fitted with a 40mm M203 grenade launcher, as well as a Browning 9mm pistol for personal protection. The ammunition back up for these was about fifteen 30-round magazines, and a dozen grenades for the launcher. I also carried a good personal medical kit and a survival kit on the back of my belt kit just in case I found myself in an escape and evasion scenario. The intelligence briefing we had received to prepare us for our journey turned out to be crap: we were told that conditions would be warm and therefore many of the guys were unprepared for some of the worst of the winter conditions they encountered.

'The intelligence on the enemy was not much better. All that was known was that the Iraqi Republican Guard were highly trained and well equipped. Despite the existence of expensive spy satellites, not much was known about the rest of the army, or its locations. Not that it mattered to us too much . . . anything that got in our way once we were behind enemy lines was going to be wasted.

'Our column crossed the border near an old Saudi fort. From the fort we could watch the border, which was one big mine field, and also observe the enemy for a couple of days. It was obvious that they preferred to spend most of their time in the trenches and did not move around much. At last, the Boss gave the go ahead and we drove down and over the border – as simple as that. We positioned the Unimog in the centre, as we couldn't afford for that to get hit, and the motorbikes were either sent on ahead or placed on the flanks so that we wouldn't be surprised. In that formation, we drove in a line and eventually picked up a track that carried us over. The bike riders did most of the hard work; not only were they there to warn us of a surprise attack, they also found tracks to keep us on route, and went on ahead to check for ambushes. Soon a routine became apparent: some of the bikes would be used as scouts while others passed messages on along the column. This was useful as sometimes the column would be spread out over half a mile, and using the bikes negated the need for using radio communications. The terrain in western Iraq was like a lava bed, but it was criss-crossed by very deep wadis that proved a danger to us. However, the lead vehicle always had a thermal imager which meant that any problems ahead could be picked up in time. Luckily, we ran into no ambushes at these wadis.

'The weather was terrible, all the more so for being unexpected thanks to the incorrect intelligence. We found ourselves driving through snowstorms in open vehicles and dressed only in tropical lightweight clothing. Most of us half froze to death, but there wasn't much we could do about it. While I was driving the lead vehicle, my hands became so cold that the skin began to crack. The gloves we had been issued with were next to useless in these conditions, so instead, I improvised some mittens out of socks.

'Our first five days were relatively quiet, which gave us time to settle down into a routine. During the day, we lay up, in a carefully chosen spot. Our lying up positions [LUPs] were usually in a depression; sentries were posted on any high ground. Also we made sure that we had several bug-out routes in case we needed to run. During this time, we actually pinged [spotted] several enemy patrols, but due to our well-camouflaged sites, they never saw us. Our vehicles in particular were well camouflaged with nets and it was under these that we hid during the daylight hours. Our daily routine consisted of: sentries out, clean weapons, send sitrep's and sleep.

'One day, however, one of our patrols was visited by a Russian Gaz 69 full of Iraqis. They had obviously spotted the LUP, despite it being well camouflaged, but, being so close to Baghdad, must have mistaken it for friendly forces. The vehicle stopped about thirty metres away, and the driver got out and started to check under the bonnet. Meanwhile an officer disembarked from the passenger side, complete with maps and charts and started to walk towards the patrol's position. The SAS opened fire and in the mayhem that ensued, only one Iraqi was left alive. The remaining Iraqi told them that they had been on a recce for the Iraqi Artillery Brigade, attached to a unit some 30,000 strong. There is a joke in the Regiment that illustrates this incident. When asked where this vast Iraqi force was, the prisoner said: "There" – pointing to the west. Two minutes later the SAS column was to be seen heading east, like bats out of hell. This little skirmish had actually been quite valuable, in terms of the prisoner and the maps found in the vehicle, and it was decided that they should be extracted to Saudi Arabia. This was no easy task, for it meant that the column had to drive back through enemy territory in order to make a rendezvous point with a chopper. All the way, they came across Iraqi units; however, luckily for them, it must have been assumed that they were also Iraqi.

'A few days later, the SAS had a new task behind enemy lines. Iraq had fired a number of scuds at Israel, and Israel was threatening to join the war unless these missiles were destroyed. Therefore, SAS fighting columns were ordered further west, into what became known as "scud alley". Finding the scud-missile launchers was not easy, but we had a few sightings. Once we got the bearings of the launchers, we would then radio for fire support. However, difficulties arose with communications. The radio sets were fine in themselves, but there were so many different types, and they were either set to different frequencies, or were not compatible with voice messages. Then, once again, we received new orders from the Head Shed: we were to go and destroy a microwave communications station. We carried out a close target recce and discovered that the site was large, about a kilometre square, with a vast tower bristling with communication dishes. Immediately we set about planning the attack.

'The attack itself went well. In fact we managed to drive into the camp itself and park no more than 200 yards from the main building and tower. The demolition team went in to do its work while the rest of us kept watch. All seemed to be going well, and the demolitions team were withdrawing, when a group of Iraqis, sleeping in a truck, woke up and were about to sound the alarm. We had no choice but to waste them. This was the signal for all hell to break loose, but luckily for us, the sleepy Iraqis thought that they were in the middle of an air attack and most of their fire went upwards. At that moment the explosives did their work on the tower and we made a run for the vehicles. The team leader, in the front vehicle, took a fix on a point with his GPS and pointed in that direction: "Punch me a hole that way," he ordered. Opening up with heavy machine-guns, we cleared a lane out of the immediate vicinity, but still spent the next hour running the gauntlet of Iraqi soldiers. Then, once more, we disappeared into the empty darkness of the desert.'

As a result of weeks behind Iraqi lines, the squadron received: one Distinguished Service Medal; two Military Crosses; four Military Medals; four Mentions in Dispatches. Two were killed and one was captured.

SUMMARY

It is difficult to define what motivates a soldier to attend SAS selection. Many people in society feel that those who volunteer have something to prove, or that they want to enter into a world of daring-do. If you ask me, I'd say that in most cases their motives are nothing more noble than to achieve perfection in their chosen profession, that of being a skilful soldier. That, and to serve with and be among the men drawn to Hereford who have achieved the ultimate – passing selection and becoming a member of the SAS.

Good Luck

INDEX

abseiling 162, 169, 178–9, 180
Aden 3
age 16, 20
Air Troop 141, 163
aircraft assault 167, 182, 187–91
Albania 4
alcohol 4, 19, 22, 58, 138
anti–terrorist teams 3, 167–91
Arctic warfare 114, 131–5
artificial respiration 144–5
Arwen 83
assault teams 167, 168–91

beds 118–19, 120, 131, 134
behaviour 4–6, 12, 27
Belize 62, 116
belt kit 75, 108
bergen xv, xvii, 28–9, 55, 75
bleeding 147–9
blisters 34–5
Boat Troop 141, 162–3
body armour 172–3
bone fractures 149–51
booby traps 129, 155
boots 31, 35, 54, 116
Borneo 3
Bosnia 4
breathing 20–21, 144–5
Brecon Beacons xiv–xvi, 52–5,
    60, 64

Brunei 116, 130
buildings: escaping from
    96–101; rapid entry 182–5
Bullied, David 199

Calvert, Mike 2
candles 109, 134
cheating 27, 63–4
chest compression 145–6
cigarettes 19, 87, 116, 138
climbing skills 132, 162, 169,
    178–9, 180
Close Target Recognisance
    (CTR) xviii
clothing xv, xvii, 5; assault teams
    169, 170–73; care and repair
    4, 30–33, 35; continuation
    training 74–5; SFBC 16
cold 32, 66–9, 110–11, 132–3
coma position 146–7
communications systems 152–5,
    174–8, 209
compass 36–44, 51–2, 110, 112
continuation training 74–92
Cooper, Graham xiii
Counter–Revolutionary Warfare 3
courage 6–8
Crooke, Major Ian 193, 196–204
CS gas 83, 184

de la Billière, Peter 3, 8
demolitions skills 141, 155–60, 209
desert 2, 105, 114, 126, 135–40
dogs 103–7, 123
drinking 53, 111, 138

Elan Valley 55, 58, 59
equipment: assault teams 170–6, 182–6; initial selection xv, xvii, 54–5; jungle training 63; medical 186; observation 90–91, 185; OPS 185–6; rapid entry 182–5; survival 64, 69, 108–14
escaping capture xvii, 95–108
exercise programme 19, 20–7
explosives 155–60
exposure 65–9

Falklands War 3, 89, 159–60
fast roping equipment 179–80
fatigue 66, 68
fear, dealing with 94–5
feet, care of 22, 33–5
Felon, Peter 200
fences, escaping 99–102
fires 72, 73, 109, 113, 119, 133
fishing tackle 112
fitness 16–35
flares 112
food 16, 18–19, 53
Forest of Dean 55, 57, 64
forest shelters 71; see also jungle
frostbite 66–8, 110

Gambia 192–204
GPS (Global Positioning System) 44–6, 136
grapnel launcher 179–80
grasslands 72, 126
grenade throwers 76, 82–3

Gulf War 3–4, 12, 82, 89, 135, 204–10
gunshot wounds 151–2

hammock 118–19, 120, 131
heat exhaustion 32–3, 69–70
hides 88–90
hostage releases 85–6, 169, 182, 187–91, 199
Hunter, Gary xvii–xix
hygiene 30, 32, 88, 117
hypothermia 66, 68–9, 110

individual skills 141–62
industrial sabotage 158–9
initial selection 52–62
injuries 142–52, 186
intelligence systems 185

Jawara, Sir Dawda 193, 194, 196, 202, 203
jogging 22
jungle 62–3, 114, 115–31

Kealy, Capt. Mike 9
kit see equipment
knives 111

ladders 180–81, 182
laser projectors 90, 159
Lee, Clive 198, 199, 200
linguists 141, 160–62
Long Drag xvi–xvii

machine–guns 82
Malaya 2, 116, 161
maps xiii, xx, 36–44, 55
march xv, xvi, 23
Mayne, Paddy 1–2
medical equipment 113, 186
medics 141, 142–52
Mirbat, battle of 8–12, 76

Mobility Troop 141, 165–6, 205
Mogadishu 187–91, 199
moon, navigation by 50
Mountain Troop 141, 162

navigation: with compass 38,
    40–44; without compass
    46–52, 110, 112; direction
    finding 51; GPS 446; map
reading 36–44
needle 51, 110
N'Gom, Lt Col Abdourah–man
    198, 199, 200, 202
night vision systems 90, 185
N'Jie, Lady Chilel 199, 201, 202
North 41, 42–4, 46
Northern Ireland 3, 91–2
Norway 131, 132, 153, 161

observation posts (OP) 86–92,
    134
Oman 3, 8–12, 135, 136
Operations Planning System
    (OPS) 185–6
orienteering 23

pain, dealing with 94–5
parachute cord 112
parachuting xviii, 163–5
patrol, four–man 2, 86, 141
pay xxi
pistols 78
Point to Point xv
prisoner of war 93–4, 95–7

radios 152–4, 175–7
Radnor Forest 55, 56, 57
rapid entry equipment 182–5
razor blades 112
respirators 169, 174
rifles 76–8, 83, 169
rivers 121–2

rocket launcher 81–2
ropes 112, 178–80
Rose, Lt Col Michael 192–3
rucksack see bergen
running 22–3

salt 70, 138
Sanyang, Kukoi Samba 195, 199,
    202
SAS: history 1–12; squadrons
    141–66
SAS – Are You Tough Enough?
    xiii–xxi
saws 111
selection: basis of system xiii, xx;
    continuation training 74–92;
    cost of xiii; initial selection
    52–62; jungle training 62–3;
    lost procedure 64–5; navigation
    36–52; preparation for 13–35
shooting skills 84–6
shotguns 84
signallers 75, 141, 152–4
skiing 132, 162
snares 111
snipers 83, 167, 169, 176–8
snow shelters 72–3, 133–5
solar still 139–40
Special Forces Briefing Course
    13–17, 22, 27–8
Standard Operating Procedures
    (SOP) 75
stars, navigating by 48–50
Stirling, David 1
Stone, Eddie xiv–xviii
stun grenades 84
sub–machine guns 78–81, 168
surveillance xviii, 90–91, 185
survival: equipment 64, 69,
    90–91, 102, 108–14; shelters
    70–73, 117–19, 133–5, 136,
    137; training 93–114

swimming test xviii

target recce 156, 209
tents 133
thermal imagers 91, 206, 207
tracking: by dogs 103–7, 123;
    devices xv, 44–6, 136; jungle
    techniques 123–30
troop skills 162–7
tunnels 101

vehicles 2, 154, 165–6, 182, 205
voice projection units 174

walls: escaping 97–9; rapid entry
    182–5
warm–up exercises 20–21
watch, navigating by 47
water 53, 111, 138–40
weapons xiii, xix, 75–86, 159,
    165, 168–9, 205–6
white–outs 134
wind, navigation by 51
wind-chill 66, 70, 133
Woodhouse, John 2